Praise for
101 Bible Questions

"Andrew Farley's *101 Bible Questions* fearlessly tackles challenging passages and offers a profound understanding of God's love and forgiveness. Prepare to have your preconceived notions shattered as you witness the puzzle pieces of God's grace falling into place. This book makes every verse come alive with new meaning and significance. I urge you to grab a copy, devour its pages, and prepare to have your faith reignited and your understanding deepened."

—**Bart Millard,** singer/songwriter for MercyMe

101 Bible Questions

101 Bible Questions

And the Surprising Answers You May Not Hear in Church!

Andrew Farley

SALEM BOOKS

an imprint of Regnery Publishing
Washington, D.C.

Salem Books™ is a trademark of Salem Communications
Holding Corporation.
Regnery® and its colophon are registered trademarks of
Salem Communications Holding Corporation.

Cataloging-in-Publication data on file with the Library of Congress.

ISBN: 978-1-68451-129-7
eISBN: 978-1-68451-476-2

Published in the United States by
Salem Books
An Imprint of Regnery Publishing
A Division of Salem Media Group
Washington, D.C.
www.SalemBooks.com

Manufactured in the United States of America

10 9 8 7 6 5 4 3 2 1

Books are available in quantity for promotional or premium use.
For information on discounts and terms, please visit our website:
www.SalemBooks.com.

This book is dedicated to

our amazing team at BibleQuestions.com

CONTENTS

CONTENTS

Foreword

It is with great pleasure and admiration that I write this foreword for Andrew Farley's extraordinary book. Andrew's profound worldwide impact is felt through his website, BibleQuestions.com, where people from more than a hundred countries receive sound scriptural answers to their pressing questions. As the creator of BibleQuestions.com, Andrew's use of technology has resulted in grace-based answers being instantly available in dozens of languages—a world mission in itself!

Over the years, Andrew and I have developed a deep friendship, sharing countless moments of camaraderie, laughter, and support. We have stood together on stages, served on boards, and explored life's challenges side by side. One cherished tradition among our close circle of friends and fellow authors is our gatherings in Texas, where we engage in spirited rounds of golf, delicious meals, and profound conversations that often extend late into the evening.

Andrew's commitment to his craft is awe-inspiring. Six days a week, regardless of his location, he fearlessly broadcasts his radio show in real time. I have had the privilege of listening to many of these programs and have always been captivated by his ability to offer concise and insightful answers to even the most difficult questions. His responses are firmly grounded in Scripture and delivered with unwavering kindness, even to those who may challenge his beliefs. It is truly remarkable to witness. Andrew's profound understanding of God's grace and our righteousness in Christ shines through as he fearlessly tackles loaded questions and dismantles long-held misconceptions. I take immense pride in the depth and clarity of his responses.

I confess that I had always imagined Andrew surrounded by myriad screens, each one dedicated to a specific aspect of his vast knowledge. I envisioned monitors for Scripture, hard questions, world news, biblical history, commentaries, and word studies. Perhaps there'd even be screens for theology dictionaries and cross-referencing. My curiosity reached its peak during a visit to Texas when I hurried into his recording studio to assist him in finding a missing power cord. What I discovered was a revelation that challenged my preconceptions. There, in the heart of his setup, was a simple table, a chair, a headset, and a single computer. On the screen, only the Bible and nothing else. It was in that moment that I contemplated a change in my own profession. Who else possesses such extraordinary focus and dependence on God's Word alone? I realized that Andrew's gift extends beyond mere knowledge; it stems from a profound connection to God's truth.

Andrew's calling is unquestionably remarkable. This book you now hold represents a compilation of his most profound insights, a collection of "greatest hits" in which he offers clarity, biblical truth, and practical applications not only to the callers on his show but also to the hundreds of thousands of us listening live in major cities across North America. Through his uncommon and breathtaking perspective, Andrew presents God's grace in a way that resonates deeply with our lives.

Within these pages, you will encounter nuanced and eminently practical responses to questions that resonate with all of us. I am profoundly grateful that God has chosen Andrew to be a voice on the airwaves and in books for this generation. It fills me with hope for the impact he will continue to make.

Andrew's ability to weave Scripture into a compelling narrative that showcases God's grace is truly remarkable. He approaches every question boldly, leading others toward the freedom, life, and authenticity that can be found in fully trusting the finished work of Jesus. His unwavering conviction that all who have placed their faith in Jesus are righteous is infectious. By immersing yourself in his teachings, I am confident that you, too, will be transformed.

Prepare to embark on a journey of faith reimagined as Andrew challenges you to reconsider long-held assumptions about the Christian life. This book serves as a breath of fresh air in a religious culture that often finds itself suffocated by half-truths and moralistic demands. Celebrate the boundless love of God as you delve into this masterpiece.

—John Lynch
former pastor at Open Door Fellowship,
president of John Lynch Speaks, coauthor of *The Cure*,
and bestselling author of *On My Worst Day*

PART A

SALVATION

1

How can you be saved?

Quick Answer

All people are sinful and in need of salvation—and salvation is only possible through faith in Jesus Christ. He died on the cross for your sins and rose from the dead to offer you new life in Him. By accepting that Jesus is the Son of God and therefore has the power and authority to save you, and by trusting in His death and resurrection, you can be forgiven of your sins and enjoy life with God now and for eternity.

Diving Deeper

The price of sin is death (Romans 6:23). But God loves you and wants to save you from the penalty of your sins. Therefore, He provided a way for you to be saved through the death and resurrection of Jesus Christ: "But God demonstrates His own love toward us, in that while we were yet sinners, Christ died for us" (Romans 5:8). By dying on the cross, Jesus took the punishment for your sins. And by rising from the dead, Jesus defeated sin and death for you.

Salvation is not achieved through good works or human effort. It is a free gift of God given only to those who put their trust in Jesus Christ:

> For by grace you have been saved through faith;
> and this is not of yourselves, it is the gift of God;
> not as a result of works, so that no one may boast.
> (Ephesians 2:8–9)

By putting your faith in Jesus Christ, you can have eternal life and not face any punishment from God for your sins: "For God so loved the world, that He gave His only Son, so that everyone who believes in Him *will not perish, but have eternal life*" (John 3:16; emphasis added).

Put another way, Romans 10:9–10 says, "That if you confess with your mouth Jesus as Lord, and believe in your heart that God raised Him from the dead, you will be saved; for with the heart a person believes, resulting in righteousness, and with the mouth he confesses, resulting in salvation."

In summary, salvation is a gift from God. Those who put their trust in Jesus Christ as their Lord and Savior are born again to a whole new life. This salvation cannot be earned by any human effort or good works on your part. It is freely given by God's grace through believing in Jesus's death for your sins and receiving by faith His resurrection life.

Let's Make It a Conversation!

1. How have you seen the word "Christian" used, and how do you think it is often misunderstood or misused? How does the true definition of a Christian, as someone who believes in the death and resurrection of Christ for forgiveness and eternal life, compare to how the term is commonly used?

2. Based on the true definition, do you consider yourself a Christian? Why or why not? How has your belief in Jesus and acceptance of His gift of salvation through faith impacted your life?

3. If you are not yet a Christian, what obstacles or challenges might be keeping you from believing in the Gospel? How might understanding the true meaning of salvation by grace through faith help to address these obstacles?

2
Is baptism required for salvation?

Quick Answer

The Bible teaches that water baptism is not necessary for salvation. It is a celebration of the salvation that occurs when we believe in Jesus and are spiritually baptized into His death and resurrection. The apostles Paul and Peter both make it clear that faith in Jesus, not water baptism, is what brings salvation. Acts 2:38, which talks about repentance and baptism in relation to forgiveness of sins, should not be interpreted as suggesting that forgiveness is contingent upon water baptism. Instead, it's a public declaration of faith in Jesus. The Greek word *eis* used in the verse can also be translated as "as a result of" or "in view of," which harmonizes with the big picture of salvation in the New Testament: water baptism was and is a public celebration of our spiritual salvation, not a requirement for it.

Diving Deeper

Water baptism is not necessary for salvation. This is evident in several passages throughout the New Testament. In 1 Peter 3:21, the Apostle Peter speaks of two types of baptism:

a baptism for salvation and a physical baptism. The baptism for salvation is linked to "an appeal to God for a good conscience—through the resurrection of Jesus Christ." This is the spiritual baptism that occurs when we believe in Jesus, as we are baptized into His death and resurrection (Romans 6:3–5; Colossians 2:12). This spiritual baptism is what brings about salvation, not the physical act of water baptism.

The second type of baptism mentioned by Peter, "the removal of dirt from the flesh," is a physical one. This is the form of baptism we see in Acts 10:46–48, where it is presented as a symbol of the spiritual baptism that has already occurred. The physical act of water baptism is not necessary for salvation, but it serves as a public declaration of faith in Jesus and the salvation He offers.

The Apostle Paul did not view water baptism as necessary for salvation. In 1 Corinthians 1:17, he made it clear that he came to preach Christ, not baptize people in water. Additionally, in Romans 3:22, Paul states that righteousness comes through faith in Jesus Christ to all who *believe*, not all who are baptized in water. This message is consistent throughout the New Testament: salvation is through faith in Jesus Christ, not through any good works, ceremonies, or rituals.

Acts 2:38 has caused much heated discussion over the years. At first glance, the verse seems to be teaching that forgiveness of sins is contingent upon baptism. But is this the best interpretation of it? The main source of the debate is the Greek word *eis* as it relates to forgiveness. Many have taught that *eis* is best translated as "for." This interpretation strongly suggests that forgiveness is contingent upon baptism. However, *eis* can be translated in other ways. It can mean "as a result of," "in view of," or "because of." It seems clear that baptism is to occur because of, as a result of, or in view of our forgiveness in Christ. Any other interpretation makes the gift of the Gospel works-based, not grace-based.

Furthermore, in John 3:5–6, the necessity of being "born of water and the Spirit" to enter God's Kingdom is often cited as evidence for water baptism being necessary for salvation. However, in this passage, "born of water" refers to physical birth (amniotic fluid), while being "born of the Spirit" refers to spiritual birth. Essentially, John is saying that one cannot enter the Kingdom simply by being physically born (as the Jews in particular might have imagined); one must be spiritually reborn. This passage is not referring to water baptism, but rather to the need for spiritual rebirth through faith in Jesus Christ.

In conclusion, the Bible teaches that water baptism is not necessary for salvation. It's a symbolic act that serves as a public declaration of faith in Jesus and the salvation He offers. The New Testament is clear that salvation comes through faith in Jesus Christ, not through any good works or rituals. Acts 2:38, when interpreted in context and in harmony with the rest of the New Testament, teaches that salvation is not contingent upon baptism, but rather on faith in Jesus Christ. The physical act of water baptism is not necessary for salvation, but it serves as a visible expression of the spiritual transformation that has already occurred within the believer through faith in Jesus Christ.

Let's Make It a Conversation!

1. Have you ever encountered the belief that water baptism is necessary for salvation? How do you feel about this teaching in light of what the Bible says about spiritual baptism and salvation through faith?

2. What is your response to the Apostle Paul's statement that he was not sent to baptize, but to preach the Gospel (1 Corinthians 1:17)? How do you think this statement relates to the topic of water baptism and salvation?

3. How do you interpret the story of the thief on the cross, who was never baptized in water but went to Heaven with Jesus very shortly after meeting Him (Luke 23:43)? How might this story impact your understanding of the role of water baptism in salvation?

4. In the early church, water baptism was closely linked to salvation. What do you think might have contributed to this association? (Hint: Consider the influence of John the Baptist and the Jewish religion, as well as the historical meaning baptism held before the advent of Christianity.)

3

Is the entire world saved?

Quick Answer

The Bible doesn't support the idea that everyone is or will be saved. It's clear that those who reject the Gospel will not be saved and will remain unforgiven in God's eyes. Verses like

2 Corinthians 2:15–16 and Romans 8:9–10 make this clear. Additionally, Ephesians 2:1–3 states that some people live in death as children of wrath. But it's important to note that God *wants* everyone to believe, and He is knocking at the door of every heart. Still, He won't force His way into anyone's life. It's up to us to choose to believe in the finished work of Christ and be reborn in Him.

Diving Deeper

The idea that the whole world is saved (universal salvation) is popular today, but Scripture does not support it. There are many examples from the Bible in which we see that a certain group (unbelievers) will perish, be punished, or never experience life with God.

Scripture is clear that those who reject the Gospel (unbelievers) are not saved and remain unforgiven and unrighteous in God's eyes. This is evident in verses such as 2 Corinthians 2:15–16, which says that some people are perishing; 2 Corinthians 6:14–17, which states that unbelievers are darkness, not light; and Romans 8:9–10, which indicates that some people do not have the Spirit of Christ and do not belong to God. Additionally, 2 Corinthians 13:5 says that some people do not have Jesus in them, and Ephesians 2:1–3 points out that some people are living in death as children of wrath. Ephesians 2:12 also mentions that historically, millions of Gentiles were excluded from salvation and without hope, while Ephesians 4:17–20 states that some people are excluded from the life of God and have hard hearts.

In 1 Timothy 1:8–11, we see that not everyone is a righteous child of God and free from the Law, and in Titus 1:15–16, we see that those who deny God are defiled. Romans 16:7 teaches that not everyone is in Christ; at some point in time, believers are *put* into Him. Second Corinthians 5:17 tells us that only those who are in Christ become new, and 2 Corinthians 5:19–20 indicates that unbelievers still need to make the choice to be reconciled to God to change their eternal outcomes. Romans 4:22–24 also emphasizes the importance of faith, stating that only those who believe in Jesus have righteousness given to them.

Every one of us is born in Adam, and only by believing in the finished work of Christ are we reborn. People who reject the Gospel choose to remain dead in their sins (1 Corinthians 15:17; Ephesians 2:1). But God is knocking at the door of every heart. He wants everyone to believe, but He will not force His way into anyone's life (2 Peter 3:9).

Let's Make It a Conversation!

1. What has your experience been with the idea that everyone is saved? Have you encountered this belief before, and if so, how did you respond to it?

2. How do the passages listed above shape your understanding of salvation and the idea that not everyone will be saved? How do they challenge or strengthen your beliefs?

3. In what ways does 2 Corinthians 5:19–20 reveal a balanced view of Jesus's finished work and our response to it? How does this verse help us understand the role of faith in our relationship with God?

4

Does God predetermine who will be saved?

Quick Answer

The biblical understanding of "predestination" is that God predestined the Gentiles, in addition to the Jews, to be included in His plan of salvation through Jesus. This means that God has opened the door of salvation to the entire world, and He desires for everyone to come to repentance and be saved. In Ephesians, Paul speaks of two groups that were predestined by God: "we" (the Jews, who were the first to hope in Christ) and "you also" (the Gentiles, the recipients of Paul's letter). These Gentiles were without God in the world, but they were now to be included in Christ when they believed the Gospel. In Romans 8:28–30, the idea of being predestined to be conformed to Christ's image appears, simply referring to the guaranteed spiritual growth of every saint, since growth comes from God. In the New Testament, we learn that predestination is not about God selecting certain individuals for salvation and leaving others without hope; instead, it is about God calling people who were not previously His people (the Gentiles) and including them in the Gospel invitation. Now, anyone who calls upon the name of the Lord will be saved, and the invitation is open to all.

Diving Deeper

The concept of predestination can be controversial among Christians, but the biblical understanding is that God predestined the Gentiles (in addition to the Jews) to be included in His plan of salvation through Jesus. This means God has opened the door of salvation to the entire world, and He desires for everyone to come to repentance and be saved.

In Ephesians, Paul speaks of two groups that were predestined by God: "we" (the Jews, who were the first to hope in Christ) and "you also" (the Gentiles, the recipients of Paul's letter). These Gentiles were without God in the world (Ephesians 2:12), but they were now to be included in Christ when they believed the Gospel.

The inclusion of Gentiles into God's plan of salvation was a difficult concept for Jews to grasp. For many years, they had been taught that Gentiles were like second-class citizens in the world; after all, *they* were (and are) God's chosen people. However, God has the right to bless whomever He wishes with salvation, and His "right to choose" is exemplified in the Old Testament through God's choice of Jacob over Esau (Romans 9:13) and Pharaoh (Romans 9:17–18). In Romans 9, Paul was simply showing the historical precedent for God doing as He wishes, and pointing out that now He desired to include Gentiles in His salvation plan. Hence, Paul was defending both God's right to choose and his own ministry to Gentiles.

In Romans 8:28–30, the term "predestined" appears, simply referring to the guaranteed spiritual growth of every saint, since growth comes from God (Colossians 2:19). God has promised that all His children will be conformed to the image of Christ in their attitudes and actions.

In the New Testament, we learn that predestination is not about God selecting certain individuals for salvation and leaving others without hope. Instead, it is about God calling people who did not previously belong to Him (i.e., the Gentiles) and including them in the Gospel invitation. This was God's secret plan, which has now been revealed. Through this plan, Abraham (by faith) became the father of many nations.

In John 6:44, Jesus says that people can only come to Him if they are drawn by the Father. This might lead one to believe that the Father is making arbitrary decisions about who to invite. But Jesus said, "I, when I am lifted up from the earth, will draw *all* people to myself" (John 12:32 NIV; emphasis added). This means that God desires for everyone to be saved and to come to repentance (2 Peter 3:9). Jesus died for the sins of the whole world (1 John 2:2; 2 Corinthians 5:19), and God loves the whole world (John 3:16). He wants none to perish (2 Peter 3:9) but all to be saved (1 Timothy 2:4).

Therefore, God has not predetermined certain individuals to be saved, leaving others without hope. If that were the case, it would be impossible for you to know if you have been saved or "chosen." Additionally, everyone's destiny would be predetermined, rendering evangelism and world missions pointless. However, the opposite is true: In the Scriptures, we see the apostles imploring anyone and everyone to "not harden your hearts" (Hebrews 3:15) and to "be reconciled to God" (2 Corinthians 5:20). This shows that the choice to accept or reject the Gospel invitation lies with each individual, and the invitation is open to all (Romans 10:13).

In conclusion, the concept of predestination is about God's secret plan (now revealed!) to extend the Gospel to everyone in the world so that anyone can call on the name of the Lord and be saved. So let's share the good news of the Gospel with all people, knowing that salvation is an open invitation to everyone (Romans 10:13).

Let's Make It a Conversation!

1. What is your understanding of predestination? Have you ever heard the view that it refers to God's secret plan, now revealed, to include the Gentiles in the Gospel invitation?
2. How does the idea that God loves the world and wants all people to be saved affect your understanding of predestination?
3. Some argue that if God truly wanted everyone to be saved, then everyone would be saved already. How do you respond to this viewpoint, considering factors such as Satan's fall from Heaven, the disobedience of Adam and Eve, and widespread disobedience among humans in general?
4. Which view of God do you think is greater: a God who controls all of our decisions or a God who remains sovereign despite our choices? Explain your reasoning.

5

Can a spiritually dead person respond to the Gospel?

Quick Answer

The idea that people who are spiritually dead cannot call upon the Lord for salvation contradicts what Scripture teaches. God invites all people everywhere to believe in His Son. The idea that humans cannot believe in Jesus because of their spiritually dead state is not biblical. Passages like Romans 3:10–12 describe the condition of humanity due to sin, but do not say that people are unable to believe in Jesus. Romans 10:13 states that all who call on the name of the Lord will be saved. God wants all people to be saved and has extended to everyone an invitation to receive Jesus. This invitation can be rejected or accepted by anyone.

Diving Deeper

The theology of Calvinism and Reformed thinking posits that people who are spiritually dead cannot call upon the Lord for salvation. However, this contradicts what Scripture teaches. The Bible clearly states that God is inviting all people every-where to believe in His Son (Romans 10:13; John 3:16; 2 Peter 3:9). The idea that humans cannot believe in Jesus because of their spiritually dead state is not supported by the Bible.

Some point to verses like Romans 3:10–12 as evidence for the idea that spiritually dead people cannot believe in Jesus. However, these verses only describe the condition of humanity due to sin: that nobody knows or seeks God. They do not say that people are unable to call upon Him once they hear the Gospel. In fact, Romans 10:13 states that all who call on the name of the Lord will be saved, depicting a wide-open Gospel invitation. This message of salvation through faith in Jesus is repeated throughout Scripture, with no caveats or conditions attached.

Scripture teaches that spiritual deadness does not prevent people from believing in Jesus. God wants all people to be saved and has extended an invitation to receive Jesus (2 Peter 3:9; 1 Timothy 2:4). Some might point to John 6:44, which says no one comes to Jesus unless God draws them, but John 12:32 indicates that God is drawing all people unto Himself. This invitation is legitimate and can be rejected or embraced by people. When we do believe in Jesus, we are given new spirits through the regenerating power of the Holy Spirit (Titus 3:5). Our new spirits permanently believe in Jesus and love Him with an undying love (Romans 6:17; Ephesians 6:24).

In conclusion, the Bible teaches that all people, regardless of their spiritual state, have the capacity to believe in Jesus and receive salvation. God has extended a wide-open invitation to all, and it is up to us to accept or reject it. The idea that spiritually dead people cannot call upon the Lord for salvation is simply not supported by Scripture.

Let's Make it a Conversation!

1. How does the idea that spiritually dead people cannot believe in Jesus contradict scriptural teachings about God's

invitation for salvation? How could this belief limit the understanding of God's grace and mercy?

2. How does Romans 10:13 depict the possibility of salvation? How does it refute the idea that spiritually dead people cannot believe in Jesus?

3. Can you find verses in the Bible that support the idea that any person, regardless of their spiritual state, has the capacity to believe in Jesus and receive salvation? How do these verses demonstrate God's wide-open invitation for salvation? How do these passages challenge the idea that spiritually dead people cannot believe in Jesus?

6

Why does James 2 state that one is "justified by works"?

Quick Answer

James 2 does not conflict with the doctrine of justification by faith alone, but emphasizes the importance of a living faith that includes a response to God's message, rather than just an intellectual agreement with the facts. James is encouraging his readers to follow the examples of Abraham and Rahab, who made a one-time decision in response to God's message as a demonstration of their living faith. In this way, James is emphasizing that true faith is more than just a mental acknowledgement of some facts; it requires responding to the Gospel by opening the door of your life and offering yourself to Jesus Christ. Jesus taught this same concept in John 6:29

when He said, "This is the work of God, that you believe..."
The so-called "work" is to believe.

Diving Deeper

James 2 is a passage that has caused confusion and contro-
versy for many people, particularly due to its statements that
we are "justified by works." At first glance, these statements
may seem to contradict the idea that we are justified by faith
alone. However, upon closer examination, it becomes clear
that James is not talking about works as a lifelong track record
of good deeds, but rather about a specific decision in response
to God's message.

Three different times, the passage states that we are "justified by works":

1. "Was our father Abraham not justified by works when he
   offered up his son Isaac on the altar?" (James 2:21)
2. "You see that a person is justified by works and not by faith
   alone." (James 2:24)
3. "In the same way, was Rahab the prostitute not justified
   by works also when she received the messengers and sent
   them out by another way?" (James 2:25)

Fortunately, James provides three examples of what he
means by "works" in the passage: offering what is needed,
offering someone as a sacrifice (as Abraham did with Isaac),
and opening the door to the spies (as Rahab did). In each

case, these works are not ongoing efforts to earn salvation, but rather one-time decisions made in response to God's message. They are not about earning God's favor, but rather about expressing faith in Him.

It is important to note that James is not introducing a new doctrine of justification but emphasizing the importance of a living faith that includes a response to God's message. This is consistent with the paradox Jesus taught when He said: "This is the work of God, that you believe in Him whom He has sent" (John 6:29). James is contrasting the living faith that saves versus the dead faith of demons who "believe" in God (James 2:19).

Some have attempted to explain this challenging passage by purporting that James is not talking about being justified before God, but being justified before men. While this is a creative take, there is simply no support for this view in the passage itself. In fact, it is salvation itself (justification before God) that is clearly in focus throughout the passage, and there is no mention at all of getting right before men:

"Can that faith save him?" (James 2:14)

"Abraham believed God, and it was credited to him as righteousness." (James 2:23 NIV)

Keep in mind that this passage is not about works after salvation, as so many popular theologians claim. Without a doubt, James is talking about what kind of active-faith-with-response saves a person and makes him or her righteous. His point is simply that there is a living faith that involves opening the door of our lives (just like Rahab opened the door) and offering ourselves to God (just like Abraham offered Isaac). This one-time decision to call upon the Lord is the response to the Gospel that truly saves.

In summary, James is not saying that we can earn our salvation through our own efforts. This would contradict the clear teaching of Scripture that salvation is a gift of grace, received through faith in Jesus Christ (Ephesians 2:8–9). James is not saying that works are necessary for salvation, but rather that an actual personal response to the Gospel is required. James is contrasting living faith, which involves such a response, with dead faith like the demons have: they believe in God, but do not respond to His message.

Let's Make It a Conversation!

1. What is your understanding of the meaning of faith and works as described in James 2?
2. How do the examples of Abraham and Rahab in this passage illustrate James's point about the nature of true, living faith?
3. How do you respond to the idea that the only "work" God requires is belief in Jesus, as stated in John 6:29?
4. Based on your understanding of this passage, do you believe that you have a "living" faith? Why or why not?

7
What is the narrow gate that leads to life?

Quick Answer

Religion teaches salvation through good works, but Christianity offers something unique: grace. Grace means that salvation is based on the finished work of Jesus Christ, and all one needs to do is believe in Him. But Christianity's narrow gate of grace is often missed, because it seems too good to be true. Many choose the wide gate of trying to save themselves through their own efforts, but the Law shows that this path is futile. God gave the Law to show the need for grace and the ultimate gift of eternal life freely available through the sacrifice of Jesus Christ. This is not cheap grace: Jesus paid the ultimate price for it, but it's totally free to us!

Diving Deeper

The religions of the world often teach that salvation is earned through good works or personal achievement. For example, in Islam, the hope is that our good deeds will outweigh our bad deeds on the Day of Judgment. In Buddhism, salvation is attained through enlightenment or nirvana, which may take many lifetimes to achieve.

Christianity, however, teaches that salvation is based solely on the finished work of Jesus Christ and that it's a free gift that must simply be received (John 3:16–17). We cannot earn our way to salvation through our own efforts or good works.

Instead, we must humble ourselves and admit our need for grace (James 4:6). We are made righteous through faith in Jesus (2 Corinthians 5:21) as we receive the free gift of righteousness (Romans 5:17).

This narrow gate of grace is often missed, because it seems too good to be true and because we are naturally inclined toward trying to earn our own righteousness (Galatians 3:3). The wide gate of self-righteousness is the easier choice, but it ultimately leads to futility (Romans 3:19–20). God gave us the Law to show us the impossibility of self-improvement and our need for His grace and the free gift of eternal life (Romans 6:23).

The gift of eternal life through Jesus Christ is free for us, but it came at a great cost for Jesus. His death and resurrection were required for our salvation, making it a costly grace. We must recognize His achievement on our behalf and choose the narrow gate of grace. In so doing, we receive the gift of salvation by faith in Jesus, rather than trying to earn it through our own efforts.

Let's Make It a Conversation!

1. What is your understanding of the narrow gate and the wide gate as mentioned in Matthew 7:13–14? How do they represent the way of grace and the way of self-righteousness, respectively?

2. In what ways does the concept of God's grace deepen your understanding of the narrow gate and the importance of

humbly receiving salvation as a free gift rather than trying to earn it through your own efforts?

3. How does the idea that connection with Christ is "easy and light" (Matthew 11:28–30) resonate with you personally? In what ways do you experience this ease and lightness in your relationship with Jesus? How might this concept challenge or change your current beliefs or practices?

PART B

SECURITY

8

Once saved, are you always saved?

Quick Answer

It's not possible for a Christian to lose their salvation, and many passages serve as evidence for this truth, including John 10:28–29, Romans 8:38–39, and 1 John 5:13. These passages point to the fact that God's love for His people is unshakable and that nothing can separate us from Him. If salvation were something we could lose through our own actions or lack of faith, it would no longer be a gift but something that we had to work to sustain. This goes against the very nature of salvation as a gift, and it suggests we're ultimately responsible for maintaining our own salvation rather than God.

Finally, consider three solid reasons we can know we're secure forever in Christ: First, our sins have been completely forgiven—past, present, and future (Hebrews 10:14). Second, we have received the gift of *eternal* life, not temporary life. Third, God has given us many promises assuring us that He will never leave us. For these reasons, we believers can know we are saved completely and forever (Hebrews 7:25).

Diving Deeper

The idea that a Christian can lose his salvation is deeply flawed and goes against the very essence of what it means to be saved. As believers in Jesus Christ, we're given the gift of eternal life—

a life that is characterized by the unshakable love of God and the total forgiveness of our sins. This gift is not something we can earn or deserve, but it's freely given to us through faith in Jesus.

The Bible is clear on this point, with numerous passages affirming the eternal security of the believer. In John 10:28–29, Jesus says, "I give eternal life to them, and they will never perish; and no one will snatch them out of My hand. My Father, who has given them to Me, is greater than all; and no one is able to snatch them out of the Father's hand." Here, Jesus emphasizes the fact that His love for His people is unshakable and that nothing can separate us from it. Similarly, in Romans 8:38–39, Paul writes, "For I am convinced that neither death, nor life, nor angels, nor principalities, nor things present, nor things to come, nor powers, nor height, nor depth, nor any other created thing will be able to separate us from the love of God which is in Christ Jesus our Lord." This passage underscores the fact that there's nothing in all of creation that can separate us from the love of God.

Furthermore, if it were possible for a Christian to lose their salvation, that would suggest that our salvation depends on our own efforts rather than on the faithfulness of God. But this goes against the very nature of salvation as a gift, and it undermines the Bible's teachings on the power and grace of God.

There are three main reasons a believer cannot lose their salvation:

1. The forgiveness that we have in Christ is complete and eternal, taking away all our sins—past, present, and future (Hebrews 10:14). This means there's no sin that can ever separate us from God's love and grace. In fact, God has removed our sins and remembers them no more (Hebrews 8:12). Because we're forgiven completely and forever, we can be sure that our salvation is secure.

2. The gift of eternal life that we have received in Christ is exactly that—eternal (John 11:26). The word "eternal" means to have no beginning and no end, and when we receive eternal life, we receive Christ's life—a life that has no beginning or end. This is why Hebrews tells us that we'll be saved as long as Jesus lives (Hebrews 7:25). And that's forever!

3. God Himself has promised to never revoke our salvation, and He has even reserved an imperishable, protected inheritance for us in Heaven (1 Peter 1:4). This means that once we're saved, we're eternally secure, and so is our inheritance. We can have complete confidence that our salvation rests solely on the faithfulness and power of God.

These three arguments are powerful and compelling evidence that it's not possible for you to lose your salvation. Your salvation is rooted in the complete and eternal forgiveness that you have in Christ, the gift of eternal life that you have received through faith in Jesus, and the promise and protection of God Himself. As a believer, you can rest assured that you're eternally secure in the love and grace of God.

Let's Make It a Conversation!

1. In what ways has your belief about eternal security impacted your relationship with God (positively or negatively) and your trust in Him?
2. How do you respond to the concern that belief in eternal security may lead to a lack of concern about living an upright life? Do you think this is true?
3. In what ways does understanding the biblical foundations for eternal security give you hope and encouragement in your relationship with God?

9
Can you "fall from grace"?

Quick Answer

"Falling from grace" does not refer to the loss of salvation, but rather to an unbeliever's rejection of the free gift of righteousness found in Jesus Christ. This person has heard the Gospel but falls away from it toward a works-based righteousness in an attempt to save (or justify) themselves before God. It is important to remember that your salvation is not based on your own efforts or faithfulness but on the finished work, faithfulness, and love of God. As a believer, you can have complete confidence in your salvation, knowing that it's eternal and secure. And you cannot "fall from grace" because you know you have already been freely justified by faith forever. As a believer, you have already dismissed the idea of justification by works, and you were justified and sealed by the Holy Spirit until the day of redemption (Ephesians 4:30).

Diving Deeper

"Falling from grace" is turning away from the truth of God's grace toward a belief in one's own efforts to earn salvation. In Galatians 5:4, Paul writes, "You have been severed from Christ, you who are seeking to be justified by the Law; you have fallen from grace." This verse suggests that when we try to find our justification through the Law rather than through faith in Jesus, we're turning away from the Gospel offer itself and toward a reliance on our own efforts instead.

But salvation is not something that we can earn or deserve. It's a gift from God, freely given to us through faith in Jesus (Ephesians 2:8–9). If we could lose our salvation through our own actions or lack of faith, it would no longer be a gift but something we must work to maintain. Again, this goes against the very nature of salvation as a gift, and it suggests we're responsible for our own salvation rather than God.

The Bible contains numerous passages assuring us of the eternal security of our salvation. In John 10:28, Jesus says, "I give eternal life to them, and they will never perish; and no one will snatch them out of My hand." Here, Jesus emphasizes that His love for His people is unstoppable and that nothing can separate us from it. Similarly, in Romans 8:38–39, Paul writes that nothing can separate us from the love of God. This passage reminds us that God's love is the very foundation of our secured salvation.

In Hebrews 7:25, we're told that Jesus is able to save us completely because He always lives to intercede for us. And in Hebrews 13:5, we're assured that God will never leave us or forsake us. These passages, along with others, make it clear that our salvation is eternal and secure, not something that we can lose through our own actions or lack of faith.

In conclusion, your salvation does not depend upon your own efforts or faithfulness. It's based purely on the love and faithfulness of God. As a believer, you can have complete confidence, knowing you're secure in the love and grace of God forever.

Let's Make It a Conversation!

1. How has the concept of "falling from grace" been misunderstood or misrepresented?
2. In your own words, what does "falling from grace" really mean?
3. What does it mean to you personally that Jesus will never let you go?

10
Might God blot you out of the Book of Life?

Quick Answer

Ever worry that God might "blot you out" of the Book of Life? Good news! You don't have to worry about it at all. The Bible specifically assures us that God would never do such a thing. Revelation 3 is all about how God's love for us is so great that we can trust that we're in the Book of Life forever. So take a deep breath, and rest easy knowing that God has you in His loving arms forever.

Diving Deeper

The idea that a believer's name might be blotted out of the Book of Life is a concern for many people. However, the Bible clearly states that this is not the case. In Revelation 3:5, Jesus Himself says, "The one who overcomes will be clothed in the same way, in white garments; and I will not erase his name from the book of life, and I will confess his name before My Father and before His angels." This verse offers a great deal of comfort and assurance to believers, as it shows that once you're in the Book of Life, you're in there forever.

This verse doesn't just apply to a select group of "victorious" believers, as some might argue. Rather, the message of the New Testament is that through Jesus, we are all clothed with Christ (Galatians 3:27), overcomers (Revelation 12:11), and conquerors (Romans 8:37). We will ultimately overcome all opposition from the enemy because of the blood of the Lamb and because of our testimony about Him (Revelation 12:11). Jesus is the One who gives us the strength to stand firm (Romans 14:4), and as a result, every believer can confidently know that they'll never be removed from the Book of Life.

So, in short, the answer to the question is a resounding *no*. Believers can never be blotted out of the Book of Life. Instead, we can rest assured that our names will be acknowledged by Jesus before the Father and His angels for all eternity. This is a truly wonderful and comforting truth we can hold on to with confidence and joy.

Let's Make It a Conversation!

1. What led you to think a believer could potentially be removed from the Book of Life? Have you encountered this belief in your own journey or in your interactions with others?

2. What might be some reasons people might interpret Revelation 3:5 with a negative perspective? How might this be influenced by our own experiences or religious contexts?

3. How does the idea of being an "overcomer" through Jesus change your understanding of this passage? How might this perspective offer hope and encouragement in difficult times?

4. What does the idea of being secure with God mean to you personally? How does this impact the way you approach your relationship with God?

11
Might God spit you out of His mouth?

Quick Answer

"So, because you are lukewarm—neither hot nor cold—I am about to spit you out of My mouth" (Revelation 3:16 NIV) is often interpreted as a warning that believers can lose their salvation if they become lukewarm in their faith. However, this passage is not about the dangers of losing one's salvation (which is an impossibility), but about finding purpose and focus in Christ. The problem is not being cold, but being luke-warm, which serves no purpose (just like lukewarm water). The passage is not about staying "hot" or "on fire" for the Lord either, but about truly living out the purpose to which God has called us as His children. This passage contains an evangelistic call to invest in the spiritual riches Jesus has to offer and then to find true purpose in Him.

Diving Deeper

In the book of Revelation, Jesus speaks to the church in Laodicea, saying "So because you are lukewarm, and neither hot nor cold, I will spit you out of My mouth" (Revelation 3:16). This passage is often interpreted as a warning that believers can lose their salvation if they become lukewarm in their faith. However, this passage is *not* about the dangers of being cold or losing one's salvation. Instead, it's about finding purpose and focus in Christ.

Both cold and hot water serve a purpose: to hydrate, cool off, or soothe. Lukewarm water, on the other hand, serves no purpose. So, this passage is not about staying "hot" or "on fire" for the Lord, but about truly living out the purpose to which God has called us as His children. Be hot, be cold, be some-thing—find purpose in depending on Christ and bearing the fruit of the Spirit. This is the central message of the passage.

The meaning of this passage was especially clear to the people of Laodicea, a city with a unique water supply. Just to the north of Laodicea were the hot springs of Hierapolis, and to the south were the cold springs of Colossae. However, Laodicea had no springs and had to have water piped in. By the time the water reached Laodicea, it was lukewarm. God used this imagery to show the church at Laodicea that they had a serious lack of purpose because they were distracted. They were "neither hot nor cold" and were not expressing their true purpose as children of God. In short, they were missing out because they had lost sight of displaying Jesus!

This passage is not about loss of salvation, but rather loss of purpose. Note that there's no Scripture that equates salvation with being in God's mouth. Being spit out of His mouth symbolizes not tasting good because one has lost their purpose, not their salvation.

Many of the Laodiceans were not even believers, and were described as wretched, miserable, poor, blind, and naked (v. 17). This is why Jesus tells them to invest in the spiritual riches He has to offer and to "clothe themselves" (v. 18) with His invisible attributes rather than the material goods they believed would bring them happiness. But if you're in Christ, you're not spiritually poor, blind, or naked. You possess spiritual riches in Christ Jesus, and you've already been clothed with Him. However, many of the Laodiceans were spiritually poor, blind, and naked. They'd not been clothed in the righteousness of Christ. This is why Jesus says, "Behold, I stand at the door and knock; if anyone hears My voice and opens the door, I will come in to him and will dine with him, and he with Me" (Revelation 3:20). In short, the passage is an evangelistic call to invest in the spiritual riches Jesus has to offer and then to find purpose and focus in Him. It has nothing to do with you losing your salvation—that's an impossibility!

Let's Make it a Conversation!

1. How does the imagery of hot and cold water in Revelation 3:14–22 help to illustrate the message to the church in Laodicea?
2. How does the idea of serving a purpose, whether hot or cold, relate to our relationship with Jesus Christ today?
3. React to this statement: Revelation 3:16 is not about loss of salvation but about loss of purpose.

12
Might Jesus say to you, "Depart from Me"?

Quick Answer

At the final judgment, those who have never truly known Jesus Christ will stand before Him, seeking entrance into the Kingdom through their own works and good deeds. But Jesus, in His love and mercy, will tell them the truth: they have missed the Gospel entirely and are therefore unbelievers. In Matthew 7, He tells them, "Depart from Me." This does not refer to Christians who have fallen away and lost their salvation. No, Jesus is addressing those who have never truly accepted His gift of grace and eternal life. This is precisely why He says, "I *never* knew you" (Matthew 7:23; emphasis added). But if you're a believer, God knows you fully (Galatians 4:9).

Diving Deeper

In Matthew 7:21–23, Jesus says, "Not everyone who says to Me, 'Lord, Lord,' will enter the kingdom of heaven, but the one who does the will of My Father who is in heaven will enter. Many will say to Me on that day, 'Lord, Lord, did we not prophesy in Your name, and in Your name cast out demons, and in Your name perform many miracles?' And then I will declare to them, 'I never knew you; LEAVE ME, YOU WHO PRACTICE LAWLESSNESS.'" He goes on to describe people who claim to have performed miracles and cast out demons in His name, yet He declares to them, "I never knew you; leave Me, you who practice lawlessness." Many Christians have worried they may hear these words at the final judgment, but if we look closely at the passage, it becomes clear this could never be the case.

Jesus is speaking to people He never knew—not to born-again believers whom He fully knows (1 Corinthians 8:3). In contrast, authentic believers are known by the Lord (Galatians 4:9) and know Him (Hebrews 8:11). The people described in Matthew 7 are focused on their own religious works rather than the finished work of Christ. They are so caught up in their own achievements that they forget about what Jesus accomplished through the cross and the resurrection.

As a believer, you have placed your trust in Christ alone. Paul writes, "But far be it from me to boast, except in the cross of our Lord Jesus Christ, through which the world has been crucified to me, and I to the world" (Galatians 6:14). So, it's not about you and your accomplishments but about all that Jesus Christ did on your behalf. At the end of time, you as a believer will not be boasting about your spiritual achievements but about all Jesus has done for you.

Let's Make It a Conversation!

1. How have you previously understood Jesus's words, "Depart from Me," in Matthew 7? Have you ever worried they might apply to you personally?
2. Read 1 Corinthians 8:3 and Galatians 4:9. How does the fact that Jesus knows you as a believer affect your interpretation of Matthew 7? In what ways does this bring you comfort and reassurance?
3. As a believer, what will you say to Jesus on Judgment Day? What do you believe His response will be? Why?

13
Will God ever give up on you?

Quick Answer
Will God ever give up on you? Absolutely not! God's love for you is unshakable and enduring. He promises in Hebrews 13:5 that He'll never leave you nor forsake you. No one has

the power to take you away from Him, as He declares in John 10:28 that you are securely held in His hand. Even when you are faithless, His faithfulness endures (2 Timothy 2:13). Nothing can separate you from the love of Christ (Romans 8:38). Trust in His unwavering love, and never doubt that He'll always be there for you.

Diving Deeper

As believers, we have nothing to fear when it comes to God's love and commitment to us. The only thing that angers God is sin, but if you are a believer, your sins have been removed (Psalm 103:12) and taken away forever (1 John 3:5; Hebrews 10:14). This means God is never angry with you and will never give up on you!

Through faith in Jesus, we have peace with God (Romans 5:1) and no longer have to worry about staying on His good side. The sin issue has been permanently resolved through the blood of Jesus, and His grace toward us will never run out (Romans 5:20). We are washed, justified, and sanctified (1 Corinthians 6:11), and nothing can separate us from the love of Christ (Romans 8:38).

God has given you many promises to assure you of His unwavering love and commitment to you. He will never leave you nor forsake you (Hebrews 13:5). No one can snatch you out of His hand (John 10:28). Even when you are faithless, He remains faithful to you (2 Timothy 2:13).

You can trust in these promises and have confidence that God will *always* be there for you.

Let's Make It a Conversation!

1. Have you ever experienced the feeling that God was giving up on you and, if so, what led to it?
2. Do you think it's possible for a person to do something that would cause God to give up on them? If so, what might that be? If not, what does that say about God's love and commitment to us?
3. Hebrews 13:5 says, "I will never desert you, nor will I ever abandon you." How does this verse make you feel, and how do you think it might encourage someone who is feeling like God might give up on them?

14

What if you walk away from God or stop believing in Him?

Quick Answer

God has transformed you from the inside out, giving you a new heart and a desire to always believe in Him (Ezekiel 36:26–27). As a believer, your love for Jesus Christ is unending (1 John 3:9). Through His death and resurrection, you are made a new creation in Christ (Romans 6:17), and your love for Him is unwavering (Ephesians 6:24). You're eternally secure in God's love and grace. This is not something you can earn or forfeit but a gift freely given to you. Your salvation is certain and irrevocable.

Diving Deeper

Have you ever wondered if it's possible for a Christian to give up their salvation? It's a question that often brings up doubts and fears about the devotion of our own hearts. But the truth is, if you're a genuine believer in Jesus Christ, you'll always want Him. Ephesians 6:24 tells us our love for Jesus is "incorruptible." This is because God has transformed our hearts, giving us a new, obedient heart that loves Him deeply (2 Peter 1:3–4; Ezekiel 36:26–27; Romans 6:17).

But what about those who seem to walk away from their faith? It can be difficult to know what's going on in someone's heart and mind. It's possible they were never truly saved and were simply attracted to a lifestyle of "good living" rather than a personal relationship with Jesus. On the other hand, they may have been hurt by other believers and turned away from a particular church or religious community but still have a love for Jesus in their heart.

Regardless of their situation, our response can be the same: to love and testify to God's grace. If they're a genuine believer, this may help restore their hope in a loving Father who is better than any treatment they received from a particular church or religious group. And if they are not yet saved, it may help them see the difference between "good living" and truly living in Christ.

As believers, our old selves have died and we are made new in Christ (Romans 6:6, 11). We are "slaves of righteousness" and there's nothing within us that desires to reject Jesus (Romans 6:18; Ephesians 6:24). It's this transformation and the total forgiveness we have received that secures our salvation forever. Don't let doubts about your own salvation or the salvation of others shake your faith. Trust in the unfailing love and grace of God and the transformative power of His Spirit at work in your life.

Romans 5:5 tells us the love of God has been poured into our hearts through the Holy Spirit. We love God because He first loved us (1 John 4:19). But it's not just our God-given love for Him that secures our salvation—it's also the fact that we have an inheritance in Heaven that can never perish, spoil, or fade (1 Peter 1:4). And even better, Hebrews 7:25 tells us that Jesus is able to save us completely and forever because He always intercedes for us.

So, is it possible to walk away from God? If you're a believer, wherever you go, God goes with you. You have a new heart and a new self (Romans 6:17; Ezekiel 11:19), and Jesus Himself lives within you. Your new heart is obedient to God (Romans 6:17) and will never want to walk away. Even if you try, you never will, because Jesus Himself sustains you and is always with you, now and forever. Philippians 1:6 says God will complete the good work He began in you, and Hebrews 12:2 refers to Jesus as "the originator and perfecter" of your faith.

Trust in the sustaining power of Jesus and the unchanging heart He has given you.

Let's Make It a Conversation!

1. Have you ever known someone who seemed to walk away from their faith? What was your response, and how did you approach the situation?
2. How does your transformation as a child of God impact your understanding of the concept of forfeiting salvation?
3. What does it mean to you to have an "incorruptible love" for God (Ephesians 6:24)? How does this affect your understanding of His love and your love for Him?
4. In your experience, which is a stronger motivator in your relationship with God—your own unstoppable desire for Him or the assurance that He'll never leave you? Explain.

15

What does it mean to "backslide"?

Quick Answer

As a believer, you are not "backsliding," because you were not trying to "climb" your way up to God in the first place. God's grace is freely given, and your relationship with Him does not depend on your own efforts or merit. Instead, it's based on the belief in and acceptance of Jesus Christ as your Savior. This means that as a believer, you're already in a right relationship with God and cannot "backslide." God is always able to make you stand blameless before Him (Romans 14:4).

Diving Deeper

The concept of "backsliding" is introduced in the Old Testament and is referenced in passages such as Jeremiah 3:6 and 8:5. In these passages, the term is used to describe the Jews' inability to consistently follow the Law given to them. It suggests they were making progress towards God but then failed and began to slide away. This concept is not applicable to New Testament believers, as we are not under the Law but under grace.

Our righteousness is not based on our own efforts or ability to follow the Law but on the finished work of Jesus Christ, who fulfilled the Law perfectly and secured our salvation. So it's important to understand that the term "backsliding" is not a biblical term to describe the experience of a New Testament believer. When used in this context, it can be misleading and discourage believers by suggesting they are responsible for sustaining their own salvation.

In reality, your salvation is secure and eternal, not something that you can lose through your own actions or lack of faith. Instead of focusing on the possibility of "backsliding," it's important for you to understand and embrace the truth of your permanent union with Jesus Christ. As Paul writes in 1 Corinthians 6:17, "But the one who joins himself to the Lord is one spirit with Him." This union with Christ means you are forever united with Him, seated at His right hand and eternally secure in His love and grace.

In conclusion, the concept of "backsliding" as described in passages such as Jeremiah 3:6 and 8:5 is not applicable to New Testament believers and can be damaging if used to describe the experience of a believer. It's important to understand and embrace the truth of our permanent union with Jesus Christ and the eternal security of our salvation.

Let's Make It a Conversation!

1. Have you ever experienced a time when you felt like you were not as close to God as you had been before? How did you respond to that feeling?

2. How does the idea that God climbed down to us through Jesus change your perspective on you "backsliding"? Do you find it comforting or empowering?

3. In your experience, why do you think some people tend to view their relationship with God in terms of how much they have "achieved" or "progressed"? How do you think this affects the way they feel about relationship with Him?

16

What about verses that say we need to "continue" or "endure"?

Quick Answer

In the New Testament, there are passages that suggest one should continue to hear and believe in the message of the

Gospel. This process of hearing and believing may take time, but if one perseveres, eventually the individual will be saved. For example, in Colossians 1:23 and 1 Corinthians 15:2, Paul writes to congregations, urging them to continue hearing and believing. This process of hearing, believing, and eventually being saved is a journey or progression. However, it's important to note that once you're saved, your salvation is not dependent on anything you "continue" to do, but rather it is secured by Jesus and will last forever. Once you are in Christ, nothing can separate you from His love. In short, the "continue" passages are evangelistic in nature, urging readers as a blanket statement to keep pursuing the truth about Christ.

Diving Deeper

The path to salvation is not the same for everyone. Colossians 1:23 and 1 Corinthians 15:2 both present a condition for being saved: the need to continue hearing and believing. This suggests that the process of understanding and accepting the Gospel message may take time and is a journey of progression.

It's easy to fall into the trap of thinking that salvation is always through a single moment of prayer (the so-called "sinner's prayer"), but the New Testament shows us it's actually a process of hearing, understanding, and ultimately believing in the truth of Jesus. This is why the Apostle Paul encourages his readers to keep pursuing the truth about Jesus.

This journey of hearing and believing the Gospel is not limited to a specific moment in time but rather is an ongoing process in which different individuals may be at different stages. Just like physical birth, you may not have a clear recollection of when you were spiritually born. However, Paul's encouragement to keep hearing and believing in the truth shows that he had a heart for evangelism and desired for all to come to know Jesus.

Salvation does not depend on your own efforts to maintain it, but rather, it is a process of hearing and believing the Gospel message. When Paul writes to congregations, he encourages them to continue in their pursuit of the truth about Jesus, recognizing that each individual may be at a different stage in understanding and accepting the message. In this way, anyone can eventually be saved. In short, if they're seeking, they will eventually find (Matthew 7:7).

Once you are in Christ, your salvation does not depend on your own actions or ability to keep promises made to God. Rather, it's based on God's promise to Himself to never let us go. Through His own faithfulness to Himself, we enter the blessing of being in Him. As Hebrews 6:16–18 says, there are "two unchangeable things": God and God. God is unchangeable, and God is unchangeable. Yes, you read that right! God's promise to Himself is what anchors (on both sides) our salvation forever. And once we are in Christ, God holds us firmly in His hand (John 10:28), and nothing can separate us from His love (Romans 8:38–39).

Let's Make It a Conversation!

1. Do you find it helpful to think of the process of salvation as a journey or progression rather than a singular event? Why or why not?

2. If you were writing to a large group of people whom you didn't know well, could you see yourself telling the whole group to "continue" pursuing truth and to "endure" in their pursuit of it? Discuss.

3. In what ways does the concept of "two unchangeable things" (God and His promise to us) bring you hope and comfort in your relationship with Jesus? How does it affect your sense of safety and security in Him?

17

What happens if you insult the Spirit of grace?

Quick Answer

Hebrews 6:4–6 is often misunderstood as suggesting you can lose your salvation. However, context shows it's about the Hebrew audience who were only flirting with the Gospel message. The author urges them to move on from elementary teachings and embrace the whole truth of the Gospel, warning that those who are enlightened but do not make a decision will not find repentance unto salvation in the dead religious works conducted in the Jewish Temple or anywhere else. It's not about losing salvation but about embracing Jesus as the only way to forgiveness and new life. Therefore, the warnings in Hebrews 6 do not apply to those who've already believed in Jesus. They've already received the gift of salvation through Christ and have nothing to worry about.

Diving Deeper

Hebrews 6 can be a difficult passage to understand, and it's often used to suggest you can fall away from the grace of God, exhaust the blood of Jesus, and lose your salvation. However, when we take a closer look at the context of the passage, we can see the true meaning of Hebrews 6 is quite different. The Hebrew audience is struggling to grasp the elementary concepts of the Christian message and needs to be presented with the clear Gospel all over again.

In Hebrews 5:12, the author tells us that despite the fact that many of the apostles were right there in Jerusalem, proclaiming the grace of God with incredible clarity, the Hebrew audience was still being led astray by the Law and the peer pressure of fellow Jews. These Hebrews were torn between the "Temple religion" they'd always known, with its regulations and "dead works," and the new way of grace experienced through Jesus as Messiah.

In Hebrews 6:1–2, the author urges the Hebrews to leave behind the elementary teachings about Christ and to press on to maturity. They should not try to lay again a foundation of repentance from dead works, instruction about washings and laying on of hands, and uncertainty about the resurrection of the dead and eternal judgment. Many of these Hebrews were still asking very basic questions, such as, "Why are the Temple works considered to be dead works?" "Why are the ceremonial washings mandated by the Law no longer necessary?" "Is there a resurrection and an afterlife?" The recipients of Hebrews appear to be stuck seeking answers to these basics rather than graduating to a deeper understanding of the Gospel.

The author then issues a stern warning in Hebrews 6:4–6 for those who have "tasted" the Gospel and fallen away from it. This warning is not about a Christian who has lost their salvation. Instead, it's about a Hebrew who is flirting with the Gospel message but has not made a decision yet. The author of Hebrews is urging his audience to realize that it's Jesus or nothing at all. There is no other option that provides true repentance unto forgiveness and righteousness.

The author then proceeds to talk about two kinds of ground: one that drinks in the rain of the Gospel and one that does not. This concept is similar to the parable of the soils in Matthew 13:1–8, in which Jesus teaches that some soils receive the seed of the Gospel, and some do not. The Jewish people the author of Hebrews is addressing are those who have not yet fully received the "rain" of the Gospel (Hebrews 6:7), and they are being warned of the danger of rejecting it. In contrast, the author affirms and encourages in Hebrews 6:9 those who *have* received Jesus.

Similarly, many today are exposed to the truth that Jesus died for their sins and rose from the dead to give them new life in Him. But if they decide to reject the Gospel and new life in Jesus, they won't find a place for repentance anywhere else. Why not? Because Jesus is the one and only way to forgiveness and new life.

It's important to note that eternal security for the believer is reinforced by other passages in Hebrews itself, such as Hebrews 8:12 and Hebrews 10:17, which both state "I will remember their sins no more." Similarly, Hebrews 10:14 states, "For by one offering He has perfected for all time those who are sanctified."

In conclusion, Hebrews 6:4–6 is a warning to those who are still teetering on the fence and have not embraced the Gospel. The context of the letter and the audience to whom it is written, as well as the language used, all point toward the author's intent to warn the Jews to not take salvation for granted and to look exclusively to Jesus as the only way of salvation. Therefore, the warnings in Hebrews 6 do not apply to those who have already believed in Jesus, as they have already received the free gift of forgiveness and righteousness in Him.

Let's Make it a Conversation!

1. What is the context of the warnings in Hebrews 6:4–6? Who do you believe the author is addressing in this passage?
2. In what ways does the passage in Hebrews 6 relate to the parable of the soils in Matthew 13:1–8? How can understanding this connection deepen our understanding of the passage?

3. How does Hebrews reinforce the idea of our eternal security in Christ? Can you think of other passages in the epistle(s) that support the truth that we're saved forever?

18
What if you keep on sinning willfully?

Quick Answer

Hebrews 10:26–27 is a passage that has caused confusion among Christians. At first glance, it seems to be a warning against habitual sins in the believer's life, but the author's intent is to warn against the sin of unbelief in the Gospel message. The author of Hebrews uses Israel's historical struggle with unbelief as an example and urges them not to repeat the same offense with the message of Jesus. It's important to understand your salvation is secure in Jesus Christ and that nothing can separate you from the love of God. You are called, therefore, to trust in the finished work of Jesus Christ on the cross and in His resurrection—not in your own lack of sinning—as the reason you're saved forever.

Diving Deeper

Hebrews 10:26–27 is a passage that has incited fear in many Christian circles. It might seem to be a warning against repetitive sins, with the implication that these sins could cause God's judgment to come down upon believers. But is this what the author of Hebrews truly had in mind?

Upon closer examination, the answer is a resounding *no*. If this were true, then all Christians would be in dire straits. After all, are we not all on the journey of renewing our minds (Romans 12:2)? Don't we all have fleshly ways of thinking and acting (sin patterns) that still need to be addressed? Under this interpretation, nobody would remain saved, as we all sin (and yes, we sin willfully!). Our will is always involved when we commit sins. We certainly can't tell God, "I don't know what happened, Lord, my will was not involved!"

The author of Hebrews is warning against sin, but only one type of sin is found in the first ten chapters of his epistle: the willful sin of unbelief—that is, rejecting the message of Jesus as Messiah. Yes, this is literally the only type of sinning mentioned in the first two-thirds of the letter (see Hebrews 3:18–19). The author is arguing that if these unbelieving Hebrews continue to reject Christ after they have received "the knowledge of the truth" (Hebrews 10:26), then there will be no sufficient sacrifice remaining for them. In other words, if anyone chooses to reject the forgiveness found in Christ, they certainly won't find forgiveness outside of Him (Hebrews 10:27)!

We must understand the context of the passage to correctly interpret its meaning. The average Jewish struggle was not like that of Gentiles. While the Gentiles were immersed in pagan debauchery, the Jews had the Law and were awaiting Messiah. Once Jesus came along, the Jewish struggle was not with heinous-looking deeds of the flesh but rather with rejecting Jesus as the Messiah.

This is why the epistle to the Hebrews is so unique. While letters like Corinthians and Ephesians address Gentile behavioral issues, Hebrews is specifically focused on the sin of unbelief in Jesus Christ, which was the particular stumbling block of the Jews. The author of Hebrews uses Israel's historical struggle with unbelief in God and failure to enter the Promised Land as examples and urges them not to repeat the same offense with the message of Jesus (see Hebrews 4). So the author of Hebrews is not saying believers will lose their salvation if they commit too many willful sins (lying, stealing, etc.). Rather, he's warning against deliberately rejecting the truth of the Gospel message.

Hebrews 10:29 poses the rhetorical question, "How much more severe punishment do you think he will deserve who has trampled underfoot the Son of God, and has regarded as unclean the blood of the covenant by which he was sanctified, and has insulted the Spirit of grace?" Some argue that "he" refers to Jesus who was set apart (sanctified) as our mediator and high priest of the New Covenant. Others think "he" could represent any Jewish person who was set apart (as an Israelite) to have this Gospel come to them as their birthright. Lastly, others think it refers to a Christian who was sanctified by the blood of Jesus. Even if this last interpretation is the correct one, it's important to note that the entire question posed in the verse is a hypothetical and rhetorical question urging the reader to contemplate what one deserves if they disrespect Jesus. Fortunately, believers do not get what we deserve. We get what Jesus deserves!

In conclusion, Hebrews 10:26–27 is not a warning against losing salvation due to habitual sins but rather a warning against the sin of unbelief in the Gospel message. The author of Hebrews emphasizes this throughout the first ten chapters of the book, using examples from Israel's history of struggling with doubt and disobedience. The epistle is specifically focused on the particular stumbling block of the Jews, which was rejecting Jesus as the Messiah. It is important to understand the context of the passage in order to avoid confusion and fear in your relationship with God.

Let's Make It a Conversation!

1. Have you ever believed that you might be able to out-sin the grace of God and exhaust the blood of Jesus? How did that make you feel?
2. How has this discussion enlightened you to the truth about Hebrews 10 and the author's warning to unbelievers teetering on the fence to make up their minds?
3. How is the accurate interpretation of this passage applicable today as we share the urgent importance of the Gospel with others?

19

Is suicide the unforgivable sin?

Quick Answer

Suicide is not an unforgivable sin, despite what some Christian traditions may teach. The only unforgivable sin is the rejection of the Gospel message, also known as blasphemy against the Holy Spirit or the sin that leads to death (1 John 5:16; Matthew 12:31–32). This sin is not related to suicide, but rather it is a refusal to believe in Jesus. It is important to understand that we believers are forgiven and cleansed by Jesus once and for all time (Hebrews 10:14), not through any ongoing confession ritual. This means that, for a Christian, there is no unforgivable sin. If you are struggling with thoughts of suicide, please seek help from a trusted healthcare professional or counselor. Remember, God cares for you and wants you to find hope and healing in Him.

Diving Deeper

Suicide is a tragic issue that affects many, and it's essential to understand that the Bible doesn't view it as an unforgivable sin. In fact, the only unforgivable sin is the rejection of the Gospel message, also known as "blasphemy against the Spirit (Matthew 12:31–32) or the "sin leading to death" (1 John 5:16).

In Matthew 12, the Jews were essentially accusing Jesus of doing the work of Satan—rejecting His identity and His work. Similarly, in 1 John 5, the apostle writes that we cannot pray for someone who is committing the sin that leads to death. This means we can't pray people out of unbelief into belief. They must respond to the Gospel themselves. In both cases, the sin referred to is rejecting Jesus Christ Himself. Why is this unforgivable? Because forgiveness is only found in Christ, not in Adam. Therefore, if we remain in Adam (rejecting the Gospel), then we remain unforgiven and dead in our sins.

However, in some Christian circles, especially Roman Catholicism, suicide is indeed viewed as an unforgivable sin. We may go through our entire life believing in Jesus but then succumb to a case of depression that is fatal. Then, they say, God yanks our salvation, essentially kicking us when we're down. Of course, they believe this because a "last confession" is not possible with suicide, and they presume this leaves one final sin remaining on our eternal record, preventing us from going to Heaven. But it's important to remember that we're forgiven and cleansed by Jesus *once and for all time* (Hebrews 10:14), not through any ongoing confession ritual.

Some have pointed to 1 Corinthians 3:17 as evidence that suicide is unforgivable: "If anyone destroys the temple of God, God will destroy that person; for the temple of God is holy, and that is what you are." However, this passage is not referring to suicide. It's talking about persecution against the church in Corinth. Paul is essentially saying, "Please know that revenge is in God's hands. If anyone harms you, they will have to answer to God for it." This passage is not saying suicide is an unforgivable sin.

As tragic as suicide is, God does not see it as unforgivable. If you've lost a loved one to suicide, you can know that it was not an unforgivable sin. However, it's important to note that if you're feeling suicidal, you should reach out to a counselor or healthcare professional. God cares deeply for you and longs for you to find hope and strength in Him.

Let's Make It a Conversation!

1. Had you ever heard that suicide was unforgivable? Did you believe it?
2. Have you ever lost someone to suicide? Does the discussion above serve as an encouragement to you? Why or why not?
3. How do our convictions about suicide reveal a deeper belief concerning whether our forgiveness is total or not?
4. What does it mean to you to have all your sins forgiven by God, without any exceptions?

FORGIVENESS

20

Why did Jesus die?

Quick Answer

Jesus's death was necessary for our salvation and brings total forgiveness to all who believe. Jesus's death is a propitiation, a sacrifice that completely satisfies God. Unlike pagan religions, which require actions and sacrifices from the sinners for absolution, the miracle of the Gospel is that God Himself provided the sacrifice through the death of His own Son. This sacrifice is sufficient to remove the sins of the world.

Three popular frameworks have been used to understand the work Christ accomplished through His death: penal substitution, *Christus victor*, and ransom theory. Each framework carries an important truth about what Christ's death achieved. Ultimately, the core purpose of His death was to fulfill the Law and take away our sins. And through the cross, we can die to sin and become new creations in Christ.

Diving Deeper

Why did Christ die? The answer can be found in the Law, which states that "without the shedding of blood there is no forgiveness" (Hebrews 9:22 NIV). Jesus's death was necessary for our forgiveness, and His death brought complete forgiveness to all who believe (Leviticus 17:11; Hebrews 10:14).

But the meaning of Christ's death has been debated for centuries. What exactly did Christ achieve through His death, and how did He do it? Was the Father angry with Jesus on the cross? Was the cross an example of cosmic child abuse? Did Jesus die to placate the Father or to defeat Satan? Or did Jesus die simply to bring positive moral change to humanity? These are just a few of the questions that have led scholars to consider the purpose of Jesus's satisfying sacrifice, also known as propitiation.

The term *propitiation* refers to a sacrifice that completely satisfies a deity. This was a common belief in pagan religions, in which wrongdoing would upset their gods and a sacrifice was needed to appease them. But in the Bible, Jesus is described as the propitiation for the sins of the whole world (1 John 2:2). This means that His death is sufficient to satisfy God concerning all sins forever.

Unlike pagan beliefs, the miracle of the Gospel is that God Himself provided the sacrifice required by the Law through the death of His only begotten Son (Leviticus 17:11; Hebrews 9:22, 10:14). The sacrifice of the Son of God is sufficient to remove the sins of the world. This was God's plan from the beginning and was agreed upon by the entire Trinity (Revelation 13:8). God loved the world so much that He gave His Son as the final sacrifice for sin (John 3:16). This sacrifice is different from the animal sacrifices of the Old Testament, which never removed sin (Hebrews 10:4). Those Old Testament sacrifices at the Day of Atonement were only a shadow of the sacrifice Jesus would make on the cross (Hebrews 10:1). This is why the word "propitiation" (rather than "atonement") best captures the essence of what Jesus accomplished.

There are three main frameworks used to understand the work that Christ accomplished through His death: penal substitution, *Christus victor*, and ransom theory. Some people believe we must choose one of these frameworks to the exclusion of the others, but the reality is that each framework carries some important truth about what Christ's death achieved.

- According to the framework of penal substitution, God cannot ignore sin, and therefore, a death is required because the wages of sin is death (Romans 6:23). However, Jesus paid those wages in our place (Hebrews 9:16).
- The *Christus victor* framework sees Christ's death as a defeat of Satan, sin, and death. Did Jesus defeat Satan? Absolutely! The Bible is clear that Satan has been judged and defeated (1 John 3:8; John 16:11).
- Finally, the ransom theory suggests that Jesus died to pay the ransom for us and buy us back (redeem us) from sin, death, and Hell. The Bible says that Jesus was our "ransom" and that we were bought with a price (1 Timothy 2:6; see also 1 Corinthians 6:20).

In conclusion, each of these frameworks contains truth about the death of Jesus. The core purpose of His death was to fulfill the Law and take away our sins (Hebrews 10:14). Additionally, through the cross, we died with Jesus to the power of sin and became new creations (Romans 6:6; Galatians 2:20). In sum, there are many reasons for the death of Christ, and we can appreciate them all!

Let's Make It a Conversation!

1. How do you understand the purpose of Jesus's death and how it relates to forgiveness and new life in Him?
2. How does the concept of propitiation, as described in this discussion, deepen your understanding of the significance of the cross?
3. Of the three frameworks discussed (penal substitution, *Christus victor*, and ransom theory), which one resonates the most with you and why? Can you see elements of truth in all of them?

21

What is repentance?

Quick Answer

Repentance refers to a change of mind. This can refer to a change from unbelief to belief in Jesus for salvation. Or it can refer to change from sinful mindsets and behaviors to righteous ones for the believer.

Repentance from unbelief in Jesus is necessary for salvation (Acts 19:4; John 3:16–17; Ephesians 2:8–9), but ongoing repentance from behaviors does not save a person. After all, that would be a works-based salvation. No, it is belief in Jesus and His identity and finished work that saves a person, not one's behavioral change.

After salvation, believers are called to be transformed by the renewing of their minds, which includes repentance for behavior change (Romans 6:2, 12, 18; 12:2). For the believer, repentance from sins doesn't make us more forgiven by God, but it does make us more fulfilled in life. Repentance (saying "no" to sin and "yes" to righteousness) allows us to express more fully who we are in Jesus Christ.

Diving Deeper

Repentance is an important concept in the Gospel, and it refers to the act of changing one's mind about something. When it comes to salvation, the Bible teaches that repentance is necessary in order to turn away from unbelief and toward belief in Jesus. This is the type of repentance that is described in passages such as Acts 19:4, John 3:16–17, and Ephesians 2:8–9.

However, there is a different form of repentance that speaks of regret or remorse about a specific action rather than a change in belief. This type of repentance is seen in the story of Judas Iscariot, who regretted his decision to betray Jesus (Matthew 27:3) but did not have a change of belief that led to salvation (John 17:12).

It's important to note that true salvation does not depend on changing one's behavior or reforming one's sinful actions, but rather on believing in the identity and finished work of Jesus Christ. However, after we're saved, we're called to be transformed by the ongoing renewal of our minds (Romans 12:1–2) and to live according to God's counsel. This may involve a change in behavior, but such a change is not a prerequisite for salvation.

In summary, repentance is a vital aspect of the Gospel, and it involves turning away from unbelief and toward belief in Jesus. While behavioral change is not required for salvation, it often occurs afterward as a result of the new heart God puts in us at salvation.

Let's Make It a Conversation!

1. React to this statement: You don't repent of individual sins you've committed to be saved. You repent of unbelief in Jesus to be saved.
2. How does differentiating between the two types of repentance (repentance for salvation and repentance for spiritual health as a believer) help you gain a deeper understanding of this concept?
3. React to this statement: The believer repents for more fulfillment, not more forgiveness.

22

Is asking forgiveness for each sin necessary?

Quick Answer

As a believer, you're not required to continually ask for forgiveness for your sins. In fact, the phrase "ask forgiveness" (or "ask for forgiveness") is not even found in any New Testament letter. This is because Jesus declared "it is finished" on the cross, meaning that your forgiveness is complete and not something you have to continually seek. You are a totally forgiven person, not just for some sins but for all of them. Hebrews 10:14 states that through Jesus's sacrifice, you have been made clean once and for all time. So rather than constantly asking for forgiveness, you can rest in the finished work of Christ and know you're completely forgiven forever.

Diving Deeper

One of the most amazing truths you can hold on to is the fact that all of your sins—past, present, and future—have been taken away by the sacrifice of Jesus on the cross. This is affirmed by numerous passages in Scripture, such as 1 John 2:2 and Hebrews 10:14, which announce you have been forgiven and cleansed of all sins for all time.

It's important to consider that when Jesus died on the cross, He took away *all* of your sins, including those you had not yet committed. This helps us to understand God's perspective as He looked down the timeline of your whole life. In fact, the death of Jesus is sufficient to take away the sins of the entire world—not just those of believers, but of every person who has ever lived. This includes the sins committed by people in the Old Testament era, as described in Romans 3:25, as well as the sins of people living today.

The idea that Jesus's sacrifice was sufficient to take away all sins for all time with no need for any further sacrifices is a key concept in Christianity. This is reinforced by passages such as Hebrews 7:27 and 1 Peter 3:18, which tell us that Jesus died "once for all," and that His death is sufficient to take away all of our sins. And now, Jesus sits at the right hand of the Father (Hebrews 1:3), having completed the work of taking away our sins through His death on the cross.

This starkly contrasts the Old Testament system of sacrifices, in which the high priests were never able to truly take away sins and had to constantly offer new sacrifices. However, Jesus's sacrifice was once and for all, and it was sufficient to take away all of our sins. This means that as a believer, you don't have to ask for forgiveness for every individual sin you commit. Instead, you can thank God for the total forgiveness that you have received through Jesus Christ.

So, once-for-all forgiveness is the idea that Christ's sacrifice was so perfect and complete that He only needed to die once to achieve your total forgiveness forever (1 Peter 3:18; Romans 6:10; Hebrews 7:27; Hebrews 10:14). His work was so sufficient, in fact, that He sat down at God's right hand afterward, never to die again (Hebrews 10:12).

Some popular theology suggests that there are two types of forgiveness from God ("positional" and "relational"). They claim that when we believe in Jesus, we are completely forgiven "positionally," but we need to confess our sins to remain forgiven "relationally." However, this terminology or concept cannot be found in the Bible, and Scripture does not teach two types of forgiveness from God. There is only one type of forgiveness, total and complete, given to us because of the death of Christ (Hebrews 10:14).

Of course, it's still important for you to recognize your wrongdoing, take responsibility for your actions, and turn away from sin. You may also need to seek to repair relationships with other people whom you've harmed (a spouse, a friend, etc.). But you don't have to worry about needing more forgiveness from God. Relationship with Him is different, because He is the only one who sent His Son to die for you. You can rest in the knowledge that your sins have been taken away through the sacrifice of Jesus, and you can experience the freedom and joy that comes from being made clean before God forever.

Let's Make It a Conversation!

1. How has understanding the finished work of Christ on the cross impacted your view of forgiveness?
2. In what ways does the truth that you've been forgiven and cleansed of all sins through Christ's sacrifice change the way you view repentance?
3. Does not having to ask for forgiveness make you want to sin more? Why or why not?
4. If someone asked you how they should respond after sinning, what would you tell them?

23

Does the message of total forgiveness encourage sinning?

Quick Answer

Some think that teaching believers about their total forgiveness of sins through Jesus Christ will encourage sinning, but the opposite is true according to 2 Peter 1:9 and Luke 7:47. These passages state that remembering our total forgiveness promotes godly living, and that those who are forgiven much will love much. Titus 2:11–12 also says God's grace teaches us to deny ungodliness and leads us to upright living. Therefore, you should not fear the total forgiveness offered through Christ's finished work, but rather embrace it to live a godly life and love others.

Diving Deeper

Some may believe embracing the message of total forgiveness of sins through Jesus Christ (as stated in Hebrews 10:14) will encourage a desire to abuse this forgiveness and continue sinning. However, the Bible teaches the opposite. According to 2 Peter 1:9, those who remember their total purification from sins through Christ display godly characteristics, while those who forget this purification are lacking in godly qualities. In other words, it's when we forget what Christ has accomplished for us that we're more likely to sin.

Titus 2:11–12 also tells us the grace of God teaches us to deny ungodliness and live uprightly. While it's true that God's grace does increase when we sin (as mentioned in Romans 6:1), if we focus on the empowering grace of God in our lives, we can expect to live fruitfully rather than sinfully. Jesus Himself confirms this in Luke 7:

> "A moneylender had two debtors: the one owed five hundred denarii, and the other, fifty. When they were unable to repay, he canceled the debts of both. So which of them will love him more?" Simon answered and said, "I assume the one for whom he canceled the greater debt." And He said to him, "You have judged correctly." And turning toward the woman, He said to Simon, "Do you see this woman? I entered your house; you gave Me no water for My feet, but she has wet My feet with her tears and wiped them with her hair. You gave Me no kiss; but she has not stopped kissing my feet since the time I came in. You did not anoint My head with oil, but she anointed My feet with perfume. For this reason I say to you, her sins, which are many, have been forgiven, for she loved much; but he who is forgiven little, loves little." (Luke 7:41–47)

In conclusion, there's no need to fear the total forgiveness offered through Christ's finished work on the cross. In fact, the more we embrace this once-for-all forgiveness of our sins, the more we will live godly lives and love others. Rather than leading us to sin more, the message of total forgiveness promotes upright living and a deeper love for other people.

Let's Make It a Conversation!

1. Have you ever felt like you might take advantage of God's grace and continue to sin if you fully embraced the message of total forgiveness? Why or why not?
2. In what ways do you think the knowledge of your total forgiveness can motivate you to live a godly life?
3. How do you feel about Jesus's statement that those who've been forgiven little will love little? Do you agree with this? Why or why not?

24

Why does James 5:15 say sins *will* be forgiven?

Quick Answer

James 5:15 is a comforting passage that reminds believers that any sins they commit in the future will be forgiven because of the finished work of Jesus Christ on the cross. This passage is not meant to suggest that forgiveness is conditional on confessing one's sins to others, but rather that forgiveness is already assumed for believers based on Jesus's sacrifice. In other words, believers can rest assured that they are forgiven people—not just forgiven for their past, but also for their present and future. This is a message of hope and assurance that God will always be with us, treating us as if we've never sinned.

Diving Deeper

James 5:15 says, "And the prayer of faith will restore the one who is sick, and the Lord will raise him up, and if he has committed sins, they will be forgiven him."

This verse is often misunderstood to mean that a person's forgiveness depends on their prayer or confession. However, this interpretation is not supported by the context of the verse or the rest of the New Testament passages on forgiveness.

The purpose of James 5:15 is to encourage believers to pray for the sick; the mention of forgiveness in this verse is simply an assurance that even if the sick person has sinned, they will still be forgiven by God.

In James 5:16, believers are told to confess their sins to one another, but this is not a requirement for forgiveness from God. Rather, it is a way to build community within the body of believers and to pray for one another. After all, how will we know each other's struggles, and how will we know how to pray for each other, if there is no transparency among trusted friends?

It's important to understand that your forgiveness is not based on confessing your sins to other people or on any other condition you might try to fulfill. Rather, it's based on the finished work of Jesus Christ on the cross, where He paid the price for your sins in full.

As a believer, you are a forgiven person—past, present, and future. God has forgiven you completely and justified you through Jesus's death and resurrection. This means you don't have to worry about tomorrow's sins, because when they exist, they're forgiven! You can simply trust in God's love and grace, and live in the freedom and peace that He brings.

Let's Make It a Conversation!

1. How does the truth that your next sin will be forgiven the moment it's committed impact your relationship with God?
2. In what ways do you think this truth about forgiveness might affect your behavior and choices?
3. How does the finished work of Christ help you interpret James 5:15?
4. React to this statement: We confess our struggles to others to be transparent, seek healthy community, and ask for prayer, but not to be more forgiven by God.

25
Is the whole world forgiven?

Quick Answer

While it is true that Jesus's sacrifice on the cross was sufficient to provide forgiveness for the sins of the whole world, this forgiveness is not automatic and must be received through belief in Jesus. John 1:29 states that Jesus takes away the sin of the world, but this is in the present tense and refers to Jesus's role as the propitiation (satisfying sacrifice) for the sins of the Gentile world, not just the Jews. Acts 26:17–18 and 1 John 1:9 also make it clear that forgiveness and cleansing from sin is received through turning from darkness to light and confessing one's sinfulness. Additionally, Revelation 20:12 confirms that unbelievers will be judged according to their deeds; therefore, their deeds are clearly not forgiven. While God desires for all to be forgiven, it's ultimately up to individuals to make the decision to be reconciled to Him through faith in Jesus. In short, forgiveness is found in Christ, not in Adam.

Diving Deeper

Have you heard the saying, "the truth will set you free"? Well, it's found in John 8:32, and it couldn't be more relevant when it comes to the topic of forgiveness.

According to John 1:29, Jesus is referred to as "the Lamb of God who takes away the sin of the world!" However, it's important to note that this phrase is in the present tense, meaning that Jesus's life as the propitiation for the sins of the world is an ongoing offer for whoever will respond. In other words, Jesus's sacrifice was enough for the sins of the whole world, but individuals still need to accept this freeing truth to receive this forgiveness.

This is further emphasized in Acts 26:17–18, which states that people must turn from darkness to light and from the power of Satan to God in order to receive forgiveness for their sins. It's not automatic; there is a choice involved.

And this choice is crucial, because as Revelation 20:12 shows, unbelievers' deeds will be judged according to what is recorded in the heavenly books. Without the total forgiveness found in Jesus Christ, we humans will be held accountable to God for our sins.

But there is hope! First John 1:9 tells us that if a person admits their sinfulness to God, He is faithful and just to forgive them and cleanse them from all unrighteousness. All one has to do is recognize their need for a Savior, and they can enjoy total forgiveness and cleansing in Christ forever.

So, while it's true that Jesus's sacrifice was sufficient for the forgiveness of the entire world, it's up to each of us to decide whether or not we'll accept and receive this gift. As 2 Corinthians 5:20 puts it, "we beg you on behalf of Christ, be reconciled to God." Even though God has already done everything He needed to do to reconcile the world to Himself, it takes two to tango. That is, reconciliation requires two parties. So, 2 Corinthians 5 is begging humanity not to let pride or stubbornness stand in the way of the freedom and new life that Christ brings. When we choose to turn from unbelief and put faith in the Gospel, we experience the transforming power of Christ's forgiveness and resurrection life.

Let's Make It a Conversation!

1. How do passages like 2 Corinthians 5:20 and 1 John 1:9 help us understand the relationship between salvation and forgiveness?

2. In what ways does the concept of turning from darkness to light in Acts 26:17–18 relate to the idea of forgiveness in Christ? How do these verses help us understand the role of repentance (at salvation) in receiving total forgiveness from God?

3. How does the idea of every spiritual blessing being *in Christ*, as stated in Ephesians 1:3, relate to the question of those who are still in Adam?

26

Is confessing every sin necessary for forgiveness?

Quick Answer

First John 1:9 has been a source of confusion for many, because it seems to suggest believers need to confess their sins daily in order to be forgiven by God. However, this view is not in line with the rest of the New Testament, which teaches that believers are completely forgiven for all of their sins—past, present, and future (see John 1:29, Ephesians 4:32, Colossians 3:13, Hebrews 8:12, Hebrews 10:14, and Hebrews 10:17). In reality, 1 John 1:9 is not directed at believers at all, but rather at those who denied the physicality of Jesus and the reality of sin. These sin deniers were not yet saved, and John was addressing them in an attempt to lead them to salvation. Therefore, 1 John 1:9 is an invitation to confess one's sinfulness and receive forgiveness and cleansing of *all* unrighteousness. This occurs at salvation, not on an ongoing basis. So, once you've believed in Jesus, you've been forgiven and cleansed of all unrighteousness. Your forgiveness does not depend on your continual confession of sin.

Diving Deeper

First John 1:9 has caused much confusion among believers because it seems to suggest we need to confess our sins daily in order to be forgiven by God. However, this view is not supported by the rest of the New Testament, which announces believers are totally forgiven for all sins forever (see John 1:29, Ephesians 4:32, Colossians 3:13, Hebrews 8:12, Hebrews 10:14, and Hebrews 10:17). The truth is that 1 John 1:9 is not directed at believers at all. Simply put, we cannot be simultaneously forgiven and not forgiven. Christ's sacrifice was sufficient to take away all our sins for all time (Hebrews 10:14).

If we accept the idea that we need to confess our sins daily in order to be forgiven by God, we're ignoring numerous passages in the New Testament that speak of our "once for all" forgiveness in Jesus. We would be disregarding these passages and claiming we need to confess each and every sin in order to "activate" or "appropriate" God's forgiveness. But the truth is simple and powerful: We believers are totally forgiven people—past, present, and future—no matter what.

First John 1:9 is an invitation to the sin denier to acknowledge their sinfulness and be forgiven and cleansed of all unrighteousness. This happens at salvation. When we confess our sinfulness and trust Jesus to save us, we are forgiven and cleansed of *all* unrighteousness. This forgiveness totally depends on the finished work of Christ, not any ongoing confession of sins to God.

It's important to remember that 1 John 1 is directed at a group of people who did not have fellowship with the Father or the Son. John has an evangelistic intent as he writes, "What we have seen and heard we proclaim to you also, so that you too may have fellowship with us; and indeed our fellowship is with the Father, and with His Son Jesus Christ" (1 John 1:3). In John's letter, fellowship is synonymous with salvation. John is making a serious judgment call about this particular group of individuals and declaring that they are not yet saved. He writes to them so they will admit their sinfulness and obtain fellowship with other believers and with God.

In fact, 1 John 1 addresses two specific beliefs that prevented early Gnostics from being saved. First, John addresses the Gnostic denial of the physicality of Jesus. This group of heretics did not believe Jesus came in the flesh, because they regarded the body as evil. So John uses sensory words to demonstrate that Jesus was *physically* present on Earth:

> What was from the beginning, what we have heard, what we have seen with our eyes, what we have looked at and touched with our hands, concerning the Word of Life. (1 John 1:1)

John's point is clear: Jesus came in the flesh, and anyone who denies His physicality is not of God (1 John 4:2).

Second, John addresses this same group's denial of the reality of sin. In 1 John 1:8–10, he says:

If we say that we have no sin, we are deceiving ourselves and the truth is not in us. *If we confess our sins*,
He is faithful and righteous, so that He will forgive
us our sins and cleanse us from all unrighteousness.
If we say that we have not sinned, we make Him a liar
and His word is not in us. (emphasis added)

Both verse 8 and verse 10 address someone who claims to
have no sin and to have never sinned. Clearly, this person is
an unbeliever. After all, what is step one to becoming a
believer? You recognize (or confess) the reality of your sinfulness. And once you've recognized your sinfulness, you can see
the need for forgiveness and cleansing in Jesus.

First John 1:9 is an invitation to the sin denier to acknowledge their sinfulness and be forgiven and cleansed of *all*
unrighteousness. Again, this happens at salvation. Notice
the word "all" in the passage: all unrighteousness. This is
reminiscent of the "once for all" forgiveness we see throughout
the New Testament. If you've believed in Jesus, you've been
forgiven and cleansed of all unrighteousness, and this forgiveness does not depend on any ongoing confession of sins.

In conclusion, 1 John 1:9 is not a "bar of soap" for Christians
to obtain daily cleansing. It's not a verse that requires us to
confess our sins daily to be forgiven. Instead, 1 John 1 is a passage directed at those who deny the physicality of Jesus and
the reality of sin. It is an invitation for them to come to their
senses, confess their sinfulness, and receive forgiveness and
cleansing through Jesus Christ.

This is precisely why chapter 2 of the same letter opens with "My little children." Here, John is transitioning to now talking with true believers as he tells them, "Your sins *have been* forgiven" without any conditional statement added (1 John 2:12). As believers, we can rest in the truth that we're completely forgiven for all our sins—past, present, and future—because of the once-for-all sacrifice of Jesus Christ.

Let's Make It a Conversation!

1. React to this statement: First John 1:9 is not a bar of soap for Christians.
2. In what ways does understanding the Gnostic context and audience of 1 John 1:9 help you to properly interpret the verse? How might your understanding of the verse be different if you did not consider this context?
3. How do the statements "I have no sin" and "I have never sinned" relate to the concept of salvation? Why would someone who makes these statements not be considered a believer?
4. How does the false teaching that "Christians are only forgiven positionally but not relationally" differ from the biblical teaching on forgiveness? What impact might this false teaching have on a person's understanding of their relationship with God?
5. In what ways does the concept of "for all time" forgiveness, as described in Hebrews 10:14, further clarify the meaning of 1 John 1:9? How might this concept bring you comfort and assurance?

27

Can you lose fellowship with God due to sin?

Quick Answer

In the New Testament, fellowship with God is synonymous with salvation (1 John 1:1–3; John 17:21). Fellowship is not something that can be interrupted by sin but is rather a permanent and unending connection with Christ. Confession of sins does not restore fellowship, because Jesus's blood has already forgiven us once and for all time (Hebrews 10:14). Even when we sin and grieve or quench the Holy Spirit, our fellowship with God is not broken. Jesus is always with us, never leaving or forsaking us (Hebrews 13:5). We believers are forever in union with Jesus Christ and carry His resurrection life within us, no matter what. If we choose to sin, we have to do so while we are still in fellowship with God. This is why there is such a conflict within us—the flesh warring against the Spirit.

Diving Deeper

Fellowship with God is the spiritual connection we have with God through Jesus Christ. It's an eternal, unbreakable bond that cannot be harmed by sin. The idea that we can be in fellowship with God when we're not sinning but out of fellowship when we do sin is not supported by the New Testament.

The New Testament presents fellowship with God as synonymous with salvation. We're either in fellowship (saved) or out of fellowship (lost). This is evident in passages such as

1 John 1:1–3, where fellowship is directly linked to salvation. Confessing our sins does not restore fellowship by bringing us more forgiveness. Jesus shed His blood once in order to take away our sins and secure our fellowship with God forever (Hebrews 10:12–14).

Some passages, such as Ephesians 4:30 and 1 Thessalonians 5:19, which speak of grieving or quenching the Spirit, do not mean our fellowship with God has been broken. Yes, when we sin or make choices that grieve or quench the Spirit, God is concerned for our well-being. To "grieve" means to cause God deep concern, and to "quench" means to inhibit the expression of God's Spirit in our lives. However, this is *not* a disconnection of fellowship. God's presence in our lives is constant, and He never leaves us or forsakes us (Hebrews 13:5). In fact, it is because of God's constant presence that we're able to say *no* to sin and grow in His grace.

As a believer, you're forever in union and fellowship with Christ (1 Corinthians 6:17). You carry within you the resurrection life of Jesus, even when you sin. This means that even when you fail, you still have access to God's grace, forgiveness, and counsel. It's essential for you to understand that fellowship with God is not something that can be interrupted by sin. Your fellowship with God is an eternal and unbreakable spiritual union with Jesus Christ.

Let's Make It a Conversation!

1. Have you ever felt like you're distant from God despite being a believer? How did you deal with those feelings?

2. How can the understanding that your fellowship with God is permanent and unending through your union with Christ help you navigate difficult times or struggles with sin?

3. In what ways does knowing that God's presence in your life is constant and unchangeable affect your trust in and reliance upon Him?

4. React to this statement: The only reason you can turn from sin is because you are still in fellowship with God.

28

Should you reflect on sins before taking Communion?

Quick Answer

Paul's instruction in 1 Corinthians 11:27–29 to "examine oneself" is often misinterpreted as a requirement for believers to confess and repent of their sins before taking Communion. However, the context of Paul's rebuke to the Corinthian church shows that the "unworthy manner" he was referring to was their disrespectful and chaotic behavior *during* the Lord's Supper. To be specific, they were getting drunk and hoarding food while neglecting the poor. Paul's exhortation to "examine oneself" was simply a call for them to consider their actions and practice respect and decorum during the Lord's Supper. Christians are already forgiven by Jesus's blood and do not need to try to "clean up" and "qualify" moments before participating in Communion. The Lord's Supper should be celebrated in remembrance of our Savior, not our sins.

Diving Deeper

As the lights dim and the somber music fills the room, we are often invited to "examine ourselves" before partaking in the Lord's Supper. But is this what the Apostle Paul intended when he wrote these words in 1 Corinthians 11:27–29? A closer examination of the context reveals the Corinthian believers were engaging in some questionable behavior during their observance of the Lord's Supper.

According to 1 Corinthians 11:18, "When you come together as a church, I hear that divisions exist among you; and in part I believe it." It seems that there were conflicts and divisions arising during their communal meals, with some getting drunk and others consuming all the food, leaving nothing for the poor. Paul refers to this as behaving in an "unworthy manner," showing disrespect for the body and blood of Christ.

In response, Paul instructs them to "examine themselves" and to partake of the bread and cup in a worthy manner. He was not suggesting they needed to cleanse or improve themselves before partaking, but rather to change their behavior and show respect for the Lord's Supper. By engaging in such selfish and destructive behavior, the Corinthian believers were undermining the very meaning and purpose of the meal. Paul's comments had nothing to do with believers being unforgiven or unworthy, but rather with the specific way in which the Corinthians were conducting themselves during the supper.

Some of the Corinthians were in a dire state—weak, sick, and even dying due to their alcoholism. Some have wrongly suggested God was punishing them for their irreverence, but the New Testament makes it clear that Jesus took the punishment for our sins in full, and there is no punishment left for believers (John 5:24; John 3:18).

The issue at hand was not one of forgiveness or unworthiness, but rather the way the Corinthians were conducting themselves at the meal. They were coming together "for judgment"—fighting and judging each other. This is precisely why at the end of the chapter, Paul's solution for them was to "wait for one another" and "eat at home" (see 1 Corinthians 11:33–34). This proves the entire issue was the way the Corinthians were conducting themselves at the supper. And the solution was simple and straightforward: change their practices.

First Corinthians 11 was never meant to be about a cleansing ritual to qualify for the Lord's Supper. As a believer, you've already been forgiven and qualified by the blood of Jesus. You can approach the Lord's Supper with thankfulness and respect, remembering the forgiveness and new life Jesus has brought you. So, you don't have to obsess over your sins. You can obsess over your Savior!

Let's Make It a Conversation!

1. How has participating in the Lord's Supper impacted your understanding of the sacrifice of Jesus on the cross? Have you ever felt the need to examine your sins before participating in the Supper?

2. How does the idea that God was striking the Corinthians for their misbehavior during the Lord's Supper contradict the significance of Christ's death on the cross?

3. In what ways might understanding the context of 1 Corinthians 11 deepen your appreciation for the Lord's Supper and help you to focus on the significance of Jesus's death and resurrection?

29

Is forgiving others necessary to be forgiven by God?

Quick Answer

The Lord's Prayer, often seen as a model for Christian prayer and forgiveness, is actually a tool Jesus used to expose the hypocrisy of His Jewish audience. In the context of the Sermon on the Mount, Jesus teaches His listeners to ask for forgiveness from God only to the same degree and in the same way they've been forgiving other people. This message of conditional forgiveness is not applicable to believers today, as we're forgiven solely through the shed blood of Christ on the cross. Instead of seeking forgiveness through your own actions towards others, you can look to the finished work of Christ and the total forgiveness you've received in Him.

Diving Deeper

The Lord's Prayer, as recorded in Matthew 6:12–13, occurs within the context of the Sermon on the Mount. While this sermon is often viewed as a guide for spiritual growth, Jesus's teachings in this sermon are actually meant to expose the hypocrisy and spiritual slavery of His Jewish audience.

In the sermon, Jesus introduces the perfect and impossible standard of the Law. He reveals the true spirit of the Law by giving commands to cut off one's hands and pluck out one's eyes in the fight against sin and to be perfect like God. He also declares that lust is equivalent to adultery and anger is equivalent to murder.

Clearly, Jesus is aiming these teachings at the Jews, as He instructs His listeners to resolve conflicts with others before offering their *animal sacrifices* on the *altar* and also warns that they will be held accountable to *the Sanhedrin*, a Jewish council from two thousand years ago.

In summary, these teachings were meant to show His Jewish audience the impossibility of keeping the true spirit of the Law and to highlight their need for God's grace. In this same context, the Lord's Prayer contains the phrase "forgive us our debts, as we also have forgiven our debtors." Verses 14 and 15 further drive home this clear condition as Jesus sums up, "For if you forgive other people for their offenses, your heavenly Father will also forgive you. But if you do not forgive other people, then your Father will not forgive your offenses."

Some interpret this as Jesus teaching believers that forgiveness is conditional and based on our ability to forgive others first. However, such an interpretation is not in line with the Gospel and the gift of forgiveness we received by grace through faith. Here, Jesus is once again addressing a Jewish audience in this passage and presenting a forgiveness message within the context of the Law. It was never intended to apply to believers today.

The Lord's Prayer was simply meant to reveal the hypocrisy of the Jews, who were not exhibiting the very forgiveness they themselves desired from God. Surely they gulped at the thought of asking God to forgive them as much as they'd been forgiving others. And that's the whole point!

In contrast, Colossians 3:13 and Ephesians 4:32 teach believers today that we are able to forgive others because we've already received total forgiveness from God. This forgiveness was given to us freely, not as a result of our own actions or ability to forgive others first. Now, we can forgive others to find freedom from the bitterness and resentment that would otherwise control us.

It is therefore incorrect to use the Lord's Prayer as a guide for understanding God's forgiveness of believers today. Instead, we must look to the sacrifice of Jesus on the cross and understand that we're completely forgiven people, empowered to extend this same forgiveness to others since God has already forgiven us.

Let's Make It a Conversation!

1. React to this statement: In the Lord's Prayer, Jesus presents the Jews with a conditional forgiveness from God that contradicts the forgiveness we believers have today (Colossians 3:13; Ephesians 4:32).

2. How does the fact that the Sermon on the Mount was delivered to a Jewish audience affect your understanding of the Lord's Prayer?

3. How does understanding the finished work of Christ on the cross shape your interpretation of the forgiveness presented in the Lord's Prayer? How does it affect your understanding of your own forgiveness?

4. Why do you think many recite the Lord's Prayer despite Jesus's warning against meaningless repetition of prayers (Matthew 6:7)?

5. Read Colossians 3:13 and Ephesians 4:32. How do these verses differ from the forgiveness presented in the Lord's Prayer? How does this change your perspective on the motivation for forgiving others?

30

How can you forgive someone who has hurt you deeply?

Quick Answer

Relational events such as abuse, abandonment, or betrayal can cause emotional pain and turmoil. To process this pain and move forward, the New Testament tells us in Ephesians 4:32 and Colossians 3:13 to forgive those who harmed you. Forgiveness is a one-time decision to release the offending individual from a "debt" owed to you. However, emotional healing may involve a longer-term process. Here's a suggestion for how to forgive someone who has hurt you deeply:

1. Assess the damage. Acknowledge the hurt and emotions caused by the event.
2. Choose to forgive. As an act of your will, choose to forgive the person and release them from any "debt" they owe you, even if they repeat the action.
3. Remember your choice. Ask God to remind you of your decision to forgive in moments when you need it most.

Forgiveness does *not* mean forgetting, but it does mean canceling the debt someone owes you in terms of better treatment. This enables you to move forward in a healthier way, no longer controlled by bitterness or resentment.

Diving Deeper

When we are wronged by someone we love or care about, it can be incredibly difficult to process the pain and move forward. Whether it's a parent who abuses or abandons us, a spouse who divorces us, or a friend who betrays us, these relational events can have a profound impact on us and cause a wide range of emotions and inner turmoil.

The good news is that we are free to feel our emotions and process them with God. One way to do this is through forgiveness. Forgiveness is a decision we make to release the person who has hurt us from a debt owed to us. It's important to note that forgiveness does not depend on feelings. It's an act of our will, and it can be difficult, but it's also necessary for our own healing.

Ephesians 4:32 and Colossians 3:13 instruct us to forgive others, but what does this forgiveness actually look like? In some ways, our forgiveness of others can mirror the decision God made in forgiving us. To forgive someone who has hurt you deeply, it might be helpful to follow a process like the one below:

Step 1: Assess the damage. Take the time to acknowledge the pain and hurt that you have experienced. Identify how it made you feel (e.g., embarrassed, abandoned, rejected, etc.).

Step 2: Choose to forgive and release the debt. Make the decision to forgive the person who hurt you. Recognize that this person may not have given you what they "owed" you, but forgiveness is about releasing them from that debt.

Step 3: Remember your choice. Thank God for the opportunity to forgive, and ask for His help in reminding you of your decision to forgive in the moments when you need it most. When pain goes very deep, you may need to repeat this step many times. Forgiveness can be offered in a moment, but healing may be a longer process.

It's important to remember that forgiveness does not mean forgetting what has happened. You will still have memories of the event and the person who hurt you, but forgiveness is about canceling the debt that person owes you so that you can walk free. It's not about erasing your memory banks, but rather making the choice to let go of the anger and resentment that has been holding you back.

Forgiveness is not just for the benefit of the person who hurt you. It's also for your own benefit. It allows you to move forward in the healthiest way possible, liberated from the burden that has held you down.

Remember your new identity in Christ. You are a new creation, a person who now has a forgiving nature. You have a new heart that wants to forgive others. And you simply won't enjoy peace in the situation until you do!

Let's Make It a Conversation!

1. Whom have you struggled to forgive in the past? Why do you think it's been hard for you to forgive them?
2. How has being wronged by this person affected you emotionally and mentally? Can you describe how you felt in the moment or moments it happened, and how it has impacted you since then?
3. How do you currently feel about forgiving this person? Are you willing to explore the idea of forgiveness more and potentially make the decision to forgive them?
4. React to this statement: You don't have to wait to "feel ready" to forgive someone. You can simply choose to forgive them, no matter what you might feel about them.

PART D

FEAR, JUDGMENT, AND REWARD

31

Is it necessary to fear God?

Quick Answer

There is a healthy fear (or respect) of God that is rooted in understanding His power and authority as the Creator and sustainer of all things. This type of respectful fear is synonymous with reverence and awe, and it is the first step toward wisdom (Proverbs 9:10). However, there is also an unhealthy fear of God that is rooted in misunderstanding, mistrust, and fear of punishment (1 John 4:18). God wants you to enjoy relationship with Him, knowing that He is your Daddy Father who loves you perfectly. He does not want you to be afraid of Him. Instead, God tells you not to fear, for He is with you and will strengthen and establish you. Even in the darkest of times, when you are afraid, God is always with you and will guide you through. When you pray and give your worries and fears to God, He will give you peace and comfort that surpass your understanding (Philippians 4:7).

Diving Deeper

The Bible teaches us that fear can take on different forms. On one hand, there is a healthy fear or respect of God that is rooted in recognizing Him as the Creator and Lord of all. This is the reverence and awe often spoken of in the Bible, and it is the first step toward wisdom. On the other hand, there is an unhealthy fear of God which essentially stems from a fear of punishment. This type of fear is not of God, and it's not what He wants us to feel about Him.

God's perfect love casts out all fear, and He does not want us to be afraid of Him (2 Timothy 1:7; Matthew 14:27; Luke 1:30). He wants to wipe away every tear from our eyes (Revelation 21:4) and remove all fear from our minds. In fact, when Jesus appeared to His disciples on the water, they were afraid, but Jesus reassured them and said, "Take courage, it is I; do not be afraid" (Matthew 14:27).

In addition, God wants us to work out our salvation with fear and trembling (Philippians 2:12), not out of fear of punishment, but out of respect for what He has done within us. We have Christ in our hearts, and we can consider all the stunning implications of this as we go about our day. We can be in awe of the fact that the Creator of the universe is living within us and that we are coheirs with Christ (Romans 8:17). Philippians 2 is simply calling us to work out—not work for—our salvation. In other words, work out what God has worked in!

In Isaiah 41:10, God tells us not to fear, for He is with us and will strengthen and help us. He will uphold us with His righteous right hand. Psalm 23:4 says,

> Even though I walk through the valley of the shadow
> of death, I fear no evil, for You are with me; Your rod
> and Your staff, they comfort me.

This verse reminds us that even in the darkest of times, when we are afraid, God is always with us and will guide us through it. Philippians 4:6–7 says,

> Do not be anxious about anything, but in everything by prayer and pleading with thanksgiving let your requests be made known to God. And the peace of God, which surpasses all comprehension, will guard your hearts and your minds in Christ Jesus.

This verse reminds us that when we pray and present our fears and worries to God, He will give us peace and comfort that surpasses our understanding.

In conclusion, the Bible teaches us there is a healthy fear of God that is rooted in understanding His power and authority, and it leads to wisdom. But this fear shouldn't be confused with an unhealthy view of God rooted in fear of His anger or punishment. God tells us not to be afraid of Him and that He's always with us, protecting and guiding us. God's perfect love casts out all fear (1 John 4:18). He wants us to live in peace, comforted by His Spirit, knowing that He's our Daddy Father who loves us perfectly (Romans 8:15; Galatians 4:6).

Let's Make It a Conversation!

1. Have you ever experienced fear or mistrust in your relationship with God? How have you worked to overcome these feelings and understand God's love and protection for you?

2. Reflect on 1 John 4:18. How can understanding and embracing God's love help us overcome unhealthy fears in our relationship with Him?

3. Discuss the idea that it is possible to have a deep reverence and awe for God without feeling fear. How can we cultivate this type of healthy perspective in our relationship with God? How does it differ from an unhealthy fear?

32

Does God get angry with you?

Quick Answer

Do not let the lies of the enemy deceive you: God is not angry with you. God is overflowing with love for you. He sent His one and only Son, Jesus Christ, to take away your sins and offer you the gift of eternal life (John 3:16–17). This love is so profound, it's nothing short of outrageous! The only thing that angers God is sin, but when you call upon the name of the Lord and accept Jesus as your Savior, He removes your sins once and for all. He remembers them no more. This means there's no reason for God to be angry with you, His beloved child. So you can embrace the truth of God's love for you and let it set you free!

Diving Deeper

God's love for us is truly unending and boundless. He has demonstrated this love in the most profound way possible, by sending His only Son, Jesus Christ, to take away our sins and give us eternal life (John 3:16–17). And it is this very love that assures us that God is never angry with us, His children.

You might be tempted to think that God is angry with you, but this is not the truth. The only thing that angers God is sin, but He has taken away your sins once and for all (Hebrews 10:14), and He keeps no record of your wrongs. Therefore, there's simply no reason left for God to be angry with you as a believer. Even the message for unbelievers today is that "God was in Christ reconciling the world to Himself, not counting their wrongdoings against them" and "we beg you on behalf of Christ, be reconciled to God" (2 Corinthians 5:19–20).

It's important to remember that God is not emotionless. He does express anger, but His anger is not directed toward people. God loves the whole world (John 3:16), but He is angry at their sin (Romans 1:18). Sin taints God's creation and is innately opposed to His nature. God has wrath toward sin, but He did not send Jesus to condemn people (John 3:17). Remember, God's kindness—not His wrath—leads people to repentance (Romans 2:4).

When we receive Jesus as our Savior, we are at peace with God (Romans 5:1). The sin issue between us and God is over and dealt with. Sure, Scripture says believers can "quench" and "grieve" the Spirit (1 Thessalonians 5:19; Ephesians 4:30), but this is not the same as saying God is angry with His children. God is simply concerned for our well-being when His Spirit is not expressed through us.

In conclusion, God is never angry with His children. He loves you so much that He sent His Son to die for you. He took away your sins and made you righteous to the core (2

Corinthians 5:21). He delights in who you are, and He will always be at peace with you. No matter what you do, God's love for you will never change. He will always be your loving Father, and you will always be His beloved child.

Let's Make It a Conversation!

1. Have you ever felt that God might be angry with you? What were the circumstances? Looking back now, do you still believe He was angry with you?
2. How do the concepts of forgiveness and righteousness impact your understanding of peace with God?
3. React to this statement: God is only angry at sin, but Jesus took your sins away forever!

33

Did God kill Ananias and Sapphira?

Quick Answer

The story of Ananias and Sapphira in Acts 5 is sometimes used as an example of God punishing believers for disobedience. However, a closer examination of the text shows there's no evidence they were true believers and no actual evidence God killed them. It only says that they "fell and breathed their last." The book of Acts is a historical book, not a doctrinal book. Just like the story of Jonah, it should not be used to teach that God will punish disobedience with extreme physical consequences (such as being swallowed by a whale!). Instead, the Gospel message is one of reconciliation through

Jesus's sacrifice. We can be comforted in the knowledge that God's wrath was satisfied through Jesus. We believers are reconciled to God—not based on our obedience, but by His grace. God wants none to perish, and this means He wants to save all people, not kill them (2 Peter 3:9)!

Diving Deeper

The story of Ananias and Sapphira in the book of Acts (5:1–11) is often used to argue that God will punish Christians who do not live uprightly. However, closer examination of the text reveals there's no evidence that Ananias and Sapphira were true believers. And there's no evidence that God actually killed them.

First, it's important to note that Acts is a historical book that recounts the acts of the apostles. It tells us what happened, but not necessarily why it occurred. The Book of Acts details a time of transition in the Church, and it's not a book from which we typically extract central doctrines. For example, Jesus told His disciples, "I am sending the promise of My Father upon you; but you are to stay in the city until you are clothed with power from on high" (Luke 24:49). Then in Acts 2, we see this fulfilled as tongues of fire fell on each of the disciples' heads as a sign that they had received the Holy Spirit. However, we shouldn't teach that tongues of fire must fall on us today at our receiving of the Holy Spirit. In this sense, the book of Acts is a history book, not a doctrinal book like the epistles. Just like the story of Jonah—in which God punished Jonah for disobeying Him by having him swallowed by a whale—we don't teach people they'll be swallowed by whales if they disobey God.

Furthermore, the text states that Satan entered the hearts of Ananias and Sapphira (Acts 5:3). We know from other passages that Satan cannot enter the hearts of believers (1 John 5:18). This suggests that Ananias and Sapphira were not true believers.

Additionally, there's no convincing evidence that God killed Ananias and Sapphira. The text simply states that they fell and breathed their last breath (Acts 5:3, 9). Scripture is silent as to precisely why they died. There have been cases of those who were caught in a lie and died of a heart attack, for example, from the shock of being discovered. (Note: Even if God did kill two unbelievers as an example during the time of transition in the early Church, this doesn't mean we should be scared that God might kill His own children, because our sins are totally forgiven.)

It's important to remember the whole point of the Gospel is that Jesus was killed in our place for the sins we commit. Therefore, when it comes to judgment and punishment, we can relax. The message of the Gospel is not that God wants to kill us, but that He wants to reconcile us to Himself. In 2 Corinthians 5:19–20, Paul writes:

> God was in Christ reconciling the world to Himself, not counting their wrongdoings against them, and He has committed to us the word of reconciliation. Therefore, we are ambassadors for Christ, as though

God were making an appeal through us; we beg you
on behalf of Christ, be reconciled to God.

In conclusion, we need to be careful when interpreting the
story of Ananias and Sapphira in Acts. There is no evidence
that they were believers, and no evidence that God killed
them. Additionally, interpreting the one-time events in Acts
as expectations for today is not appropriate. The message of
the Gospel is one of reconciliation, not punishment.

Let's Make It a Conversation!

1. Can you share your understanding of the story of Ananias
   and Sapphira in Acts 5 before reading this? How does
   this discussion change or add to your perspective on the
   story?
2. How do you feel about the idea that Ananias and Sapphira
   may not have been true believers because Satan filled their
   hearts? How does this concept align or conflict with your
   understanding of salvation?
3. How does the idea that the text does not state that God
   killed Ananias and Sapphira affect your interpretation of
   the story? Do you think there are other possible explana-
   tions for their deaths?
4. How do you think interpreting the passage of Ananias
   and Sapphira in a healthy way impacts our understanding
   of God's nature, our own salvation, and the Gospel? Can
   you think of any negative consequences of interpreting this
   passage in an unhealthy way?

34

Does God send disasters on nations today?

Quick Answer

Second Chronicles 7:14 is often cited as evidence that God sends disasters as punishment for the sins of nations. However, this passage is from the Old Testament and inapplicable in the New Testament era. It's also important to note that today is not Judgment Day. God's agenda is not to punish the world, but to save it (1 Timothy 2:4). The kindness of the Lord leads us to repentance (Romans 2:4). In times of natural disasters and pandemics, it's important to look to Jesus to understand God's heart. He is the revelation of God's heart and the exact representation of God's nature (John 14:9). Rather than focusing on the question of whether or not God is sending disaster upon us, we should focus on how we can best comfort and love others in the midst of suffering. We can trust that God is working all things for our good (Romans 8:28).

Diving Deeper

Second Chronicles 7:14, which states that God will forgive His people's sin and heal their land if they humble themselves, pray, seek His face, and turn from their wicked ways, is often referred to during disasters such as the recent coronavirus pandemic. Some people taught that the pandemic was America's or the Church's fault, and that if they would seek God more and obtain forgiveness, the pandemic would end.

However, it is a mistake to apply this passage to current events, because it is an Old Testament passage, and we live in New Testament times. We are not under the Law, nor do we sacrifice animals for our sins (as was done in 2 Chronicles 7). Instead, we have a better sacrifice, Jesus Christ, and are perfectly forgiven for all time. The message of the New Covenant is one of salvation in Jesus and reconciliation with God. The cross of Christ destroys the idea of "Christian karma" and shows that God wants to save the world, not hurl disasters at it.

The best demonstration of God's love for us is shown in the fact that while we were still sinners, Christ died for us (Romans 5:8). The cross of Christ should matter as we seek to understand God's role in any tragedy—and instead of heaping guilt on others, we should offer the message of forgiveness and new life through Jesus.

God's goal is not to kill people or to make them sick as a form of punishment for sin. Rather, He desires for all to be saved and come to repentance (Romans 10:13; 2 Peter 3:9). It's not fear or threat that drives people toward God, but rather His kindness and goodness (Romans 2:4). Again, the key to understanding God's character and agenda is to look to Jesus; as He said, "The one who has seen Me has seen the Father" (John 14:9b).

Jesus clarifies His mission in John 3:17, stating that God sent Him into the world to save it, not to condemn it. And in John 12:47, Jesus says, "I did not come to judge the world, but to save the world." Jesus's actions during His earthly ministry also reflect this. He healed those who were sick—He didn't make them sick (Luke 4:40).

So where does tragedy come from if not from God? It originates from the fallen world we live in thanks to the past and present activity of Satan, not God. Jesus promises us peace in Him but warns us that in this world, we will have trouble (John 16:33). Our God is not a two-faced deity, sending disaster and then pretending to comfort us in it. Rather, He desires peace and salvation for all who believe in Him.

In conclusion, the idea that God is responsible for disasters as a form of punishment is not supported by Scripture. Rather, God's agenda is to save the world through Jesus and to bring peace to those who believe in Him. It's important to remember that the trouble we experience in this world is not from God, but rather a result of living in a fallen world. We can have confidence in the fact that our God is always good and desires the best for us.

Let's Make It a Conversation!

1. In what ways is interpreting 2 Chronicles 7:14 in relation to modern natural disasters problematic?

2. How might an understanding of God's love and grace inform our understanding of natural disasters?

3. How does the finished work of Christ shape our understanding of suffering and natural disasters? How might it impact the way we cope with such events?

35

Will you be judged for your sins?

Quick Answer

Are you worried about Judgment Day? Don't be! Yes, the Bible speaks of an impending judgment, referred to as the Judgment of Sheep and Goats (Matthew 25), the Judgment Seat of Christ (2 Corinthians 5:10), and the Great White Throne Judgment (Revelation 20:11–15). But here's the great news: As believers, we don't need to worry about being judged by God. We can trust in God's perfect love that casts out all fear. When Christ returns for believers, it will be "without reference" to sins (Hebrews 9:28). The Day of Judgment will be a day of celebrating that Jesus took away all our sins and made us righteous forever. Plus, we'll even be invited to play a role in judging the world and the angels (1 Corinthians 6:2–3). So, don't fear Judgment Day. Instead, look forward to it as a day of celebration!

Diving Deeper

The Bible speaks of an impending judgment, referred to as the Judgment of Sheep and Goats (Matthew 25), the Judgment Seat of Christ (2 Corinthians 5:10), and the Great White Throne Judgment (Revelation 20:11–15).

This judgment is a black-and-white evaluation of humanity, with no grey areas. We are either viewed by God as believers (sheep) or unbelievers (goats). There is no middle ground.

Some have interpreted 2 Corinthians 5:10 as a second judgment for Christians, but this passage actually states that "we must all appear" at the judgment seat of Christ, referring to all humans.

Second Corinthians 5 also states that there will be recompense for the deeds done in the body, whether good or bad. Keep in mind here that only believers have good deeds, as the deeds of an unbeliever are like filthy rags (Isaiah 64:6). Also keep in mind that only unbelievers have bad deeds (sins) that will be judged, because God took believers' sins away forever. Clearly, 2 Corinthians 5 is simply mirroring all other judgment passages in which believers are rewarded and unbelievers are punished. And there is no middle ground.

Believers don't need to worry about being judged by God. In fact, if we fear judgment, we have not been perfected in God's love. Fear has to do with imagining judgment and punishment (1 John 4:18). But the simple solution is to trust in God's perfect love that casts out all fear. When Christ returns for a believer, it will be "without reference" to sins (Hebrews 9:28). The Day of Judgment will be a day of celebrating that Jesus has taken away all our sins and made us righteous forever.

Similarly, 1 Corinthians 3 states that fire will test the quality of each one's work. This is about messenger and message, not about the individual works of every believer being judged. This is why Paul writes, "I planted the seed, Apollos watered it" (v. 6) and "I laid a foundation as a wise builder" (v. 10). Paul contrasts his own ministry with the work of false messengers that will burn up and not be celebrated by God, as it was not built on a firm foundation.

Christians will not be judged for their sins, nor will they receive differing amounts of rewards. Remember the Parable of the Vineyard Workers in which they all got paid the same? The final judgment is a black-and-white evaluation of humanity, with no grey areas. Believers don't need to worry about being judged for their sins by God. Instead, we can trust that God remembers our sins no more and keeps no record of our wrongs. In fact, we will even be invited to play a role alongside God Himself in judging both the world and the angels (1 Corinthians 6:2–3).

Let's Make It a Conversation:

1. How have you thought about the Day of Judgment in the past? How does this compare to the view expressed here?
2. What new insights or perspectives have you gained from this discussion on the Day of Judgment? How have your previous views been challenged or reinforced?
3. In what ways might it be possible to look forward to the Day of Judgement? What would you need to believe to have a positive outlook on that day?

36

Is the "bema seat" a separate judgment for Christians?

Quick Answer

Popular teaching suggests there are two final judgments, one for unbelievers and one for believers. However, Scripture presents only one final judgment for the entire world (2 Corinthians 5:10; Revelation 20:11–15; Matthew 25:31–33). In 2 Corinthians 5:10, we all appear before the judgment seat of Christ, and it's the same judgment event for everyone. Believers aren't recompensed for their sins, because they're completely forgiven. Nonbelievers aren't recompensed for their good deeds, because they don't have any (just filthy rags!). The final judgment is all about celebrating with believers all that God has done through them and doling out the eternal consequence to nonbelievers who remain dead in their sins. But as believers, we're made perfect in love and have nothing to fear, as there's no punishment or sorrow of any kind for us (1 John 4:18; Revelation 21:4).

Diving Deeper

Some popular theology suggests that there'll be two final judgments: one for unbelievers, often called the Great White Throne Judgment, and one for believers, commonly called the judgment seat of Christ. But is this true? Scripture is clear: there's only *one* judgment for everyone.

Paul tells us that we must *all* appear before the judgment seat of Christ (2 Corinthians 5:10). This isn't just for believers, it's for all people. Romans 14:10 further confirms this, as Paul uses the language that "all" must appear before the judgment. This suggests that believers and unbelievers are showing up at the same judgment. Believers are not recompensed for their bad deeds (as they are forgiven). Unbelievers are not recompensed for their good deeds (because they are like filthy rags). So only two things occur at this judgment seat of Christ: Believers celebrate all that God has done through them, and unbelievers are taken away to punishment. There is no middle ground.

In Revelation 20:11–15, we see this same judgment from the perspective of the unbelievers or "the dead." The sea gives up its dead, as do death and Hades. Anyone whose name is not found written in the Book of Life is thrown in the Lake of Fire (Revelation 20:15). This is clearly describing unbelievers, as believers' names are written in the Book of Life (Revelation 3:5). So, we see a black-and-white judgment: We are either in or out. There is no in-between!

Once again, the Judgment of the Sheep and the Goats in Matthew 25:31–33 describes the same judgment, but from a bird's-eye view. We see believers (sheep) are separated from unbelievers (goats). The sheep are told to receive their inheritance and the kingdom prepared for them (Matthew 25:34). The goats, however, depart to the eternal fire (Matthew 25:41). We see this black-and-white judgment again: We are either sheep or goats, believers or unbelievers.

Scripture is clear that we all appear before one judgment. There is no indication that there are two separate judgments for believers and unbelievers. However, there are two separate *outcomes*. Although a believer's dead works (works of the flesh) will be burned up and not celebrated by God, believers themselves are not judged for their sins in any way (1 John 4:17–18;

Hebrews 9:28; John 3:18). Unbelievers, however, are judged and sent away to eternal separation from God.

Many have taught that 2 Corinthians 5:10 speaks of a "bema seat" judgment specifically for believers. The term *bema*, the word used in 2 Corinthians 5:10, is the same word used for the Olympic judge's seat as he sat near the finish line to announce the winner of a race. However, the word *bema* is not only used in the context of rewards but also in the context of punishment. For example, in Acts 18:14, the proconsul Gallio sat on the "bema" seat to deal with a matter of a crime. Acts 18 says nothing of reward, only punishment. Similarly, 2 Corinthians 5:10 speaks of appearing before the *bema* seat of Christ, but once again, it's not merely a place of reward but also of recompense for the bad deeds of unbelievers. Therefore, one should logically conclude that it's not a separate judgment for believers. It's the same judgment described in Revelation 20:11–15 and Matthew 25:31–46.

As believers in Christ, we have nothing to fear about the final judgment, anyway. As Paul reminds us, "There is now *no condemnation* at all for those who are in Christ Jesus" (Romans 8:1; emphasis added). In fact, not only will our sins not be brought up during judgment, but we will actually participate in the judging process as co-judges with God. As Paul says,

> Or do you not know that the saints will judge the world? If the world is judged by you, are you not competent to form the smallest law courts? Do you not know that we will judge angels? How much more matters of this life? (1 Corinthians 6:2–3)

So let us approach the Final Judgment with eager expectation, knowing that as children of God, we have a seat at the table of judgment (we will judge angels!), and nothing can separate us from the love of God (Romans 8:38–39).

Let's Make It a Conversation!

1. How do you feel about the concept of one judgment event? Can you explain your reasoning?
2. How do you think believers and unbelievers will be treated differently at the Final Judgment? Why?
3. How does the finished work of Jesus factor into the Final Judgment?
4. React to this statement: Second Corinthians 5:10 cannot be describing a second and separate judgment for believers, because we will not be recompensed (paid back) for our bad deeds (sins). Jesus took them away and remembers them no more!

37

Are pastors and teachers judged more harshly by God?

Quick Answer

Many Christian pastors and teachers may worry about being judged more harshly by God, but the truth is that this is not the case. In James 3:1, the judgment being referred to is not from God, but from *people*. Teachers and pastors are often in the spotlight, and their actions are closely judged by congregants, leading to more criticism being directed toward them than other members of the church. However, pastors and teachers (like any child of God) can have confidence at the Final Judgment, because there's no condemnation for anyone who is in Christ (Romans 8:1).

Diving Deeper

Pastors and leaders clearly have a God-given responsibility to lovingly shepherd the flock they've been given (Acts 20:28; 1 Peter 5:2-3). But are pastors and teachers judged more harshly by God? Some may interpret James 3:1 as suggesting that Christian teachers and pastors will be judged more harshly by God than other believers. However, a closer examination of the passage and other related Scriptures reveal that this interpretation is not accurate.

First, it's important to note that in James 3:1, the judgment being referred to is *not* from God, but from people. Teachers and pastors are often closely scrutinized, and their attitudes and actions are analyzed closely by churchgoers. Therefore, there is more judgment (criticism) directed toward teachers and pastors than toward others in the congregation.

However, it is clear from Scripture that all believers, including pastors and teachers, have passed from judgment into life (John 5:24). We are no longer under any condemnation (Romans 8:1). And as 1 John 4:18 states, "There is no fear in love, but perfect love drives out fear, because fear involves punishment, and the one who fears is not perfected in love."

In conclusion, while pastors and teachers may face more criticism and scrutiny from people, they're not judged more harshly by God. All believers have passed from judgment into life and are no longer under condemnation. Instead of fearing judgment, pastors and teachers can celebrate the finished work of Christ along with other believers and know that Jesus will return for them without reference to sin (Hebrews 9:28). So, they can eagerly await Him!

Let's Make It a Conversation!

1. How does understanding that James 3:1 is referring to judgment by other people, not God, change your perspective on the passage?

2. How does the concept of the finished work of Christ help us interpret the judgment described in James 3:1?

3. How can we, as a community, support pastors and teachers while understanding the unrealistic expectations sometimes placed on them? How does understanding God's grace help us to adjust those expectations?

38

Will you earn rewards in Heaven?

Quick Answer

Scripture does not mention believers receiving multiple rewards (plural) in Heaven. Instead, every believer will receive the same—"the reward of the inheritance" (Colossians 3:24).

The Parable of the Vineyard Workers in Matthew 20:1–16 illustrates this, as all workers received the same wages regardless of when they began working. This is "not fair," but this is God's grace (and thank God we don't get what we fairly deserve!). In 1 Corinthians 3, Paul speaks of something burning up during judgment, but this is not about loss of a believer's reward. It's about false teachers and the loss of their work, as it won't stand the test of time or be celebrated by God. Lastly, when Jesus said to "store up for yourselves treasures in heaven" (Matthew 6:19–20), He was not referring to heavenly loot. He was emphasizing the importance of maintaining a heavenly attitude and perspective while living here on Earth.

Diving Deeper
The idea of believers receiving different levels of rewards in Heaven, with some having bigger mansions or more "bling" in their jewelry, is not supported by Scripture. Instead, we will all receive the same reward—"the reward of the inheritance" (Colossians 3:24). This is shown in the Parable of the Vineyard Workers in Matthew 20:1–16, where all workers receive the same wages, no matter when they started working. This is not fair, but it's how God's grace works!

Some are tempted to think those who worked harder and longer should receive more rewards. But that's not how God operates. God's grace is not based on our efforts but on His love and mercy. He wants us to understand we are all equal in His eyes, and He loves us all the same.

The message of grace is also evident in 1 Corinthians 3, which addresses loss. Some people interpret this passage as meaning believers can lose rewards (plural) if they don't work hard enough. However, the passage is actually focused on false teachers and the destruction of their ministry work (because it yielded no result). Their work is destroyed and not celebrated by God. Paul says those who teach a message built on a foundation other than Christ will see their work destroyed (even though some of them might be saved). Clearly, this passage is addressing the fruit of a false teacher's labor being destroyed. After all, why would there be anything to celebrate about the teaching of false doctrine? It will not stand the test of time!

When Jesus told us to "store up for yourselves treasures in heaven" in Matthew 6:19–20, He wasn't talking about collecting heavenly loot but about maintaining a heavenly perspective while here on Earth. Jesus was emphasizing the importance of understanding that this life is not all there is, and that true fulfillment and contentment can only be found in expressing Him. He was encouraging us to focus on eternal things, not temporal things that will pass away.

In Revelation 22:12, Jesus says He is coming and bringing His reward with Him. While many believe this to be speaking of rewards beyond salvation, the context does not support this belief. Notice in the passage that "reward" is singular. This is not speaking of multiple rewards but a single reward. Throughout the New Testament writings, the believer's reward is always spoken of in the singular. We're all equal in His eyes.

In conclusion, the idea of believers receiving different levels of rewards in Heaven is not supported by Scripture. We will all receive the same reward—the "reward of the inheritance" (Colossians 3:24).

Let's Make It a Conversation!

1. What are some of the ideas that you have held about the way rewards are distributed in Heaven? After reading the above content, how has your understanding of rewards changed or been clarified?
2. In the Parable of the Vineyard Workers, how does Jesus convey the message of equal reward among believers? How does this parable challenge our understanding of "fairness" and grace?
3. The phrase "the reward of the inheritance" in Colossians 3:24 brings clarity to the concept of rewards in Heaven. How does the idea of an inheritance for all children align with the message of grace and equality among believers?
4. React to this statement: Jesus Himself is our great Reward.

39

Will you receive crowns in Heaven?

Quick Answer

The crowns mentioned in the New Testament are not rewards for our good works, but rather, they represent the ultimate reward—Jesus Himself. The crown of life, the crown of righteousness, and the crown of glory all refer to Jesus and what He means to us. These crowns are not symbols of our accomplishments but rather, they represent the person of Jesus and what He has done for us. In John's vision in Revelation, twenty-four elders lay these crowns at Jesus's feet, declaring that He alone is worthy of all honor and glory. Remember, the crowns are not rewards for our good works but a reminder of the ultimate reward, Jesus.

Diving Deeper

Crowns have been a symbol of victory and achievement for centuries, but in the New Testament, they take on a whole new meaning. They are not rewards for our good works, but rather, they represent the ultimate reward: Jesus Himself. As stated in James 1:12 "Blessed is a man who perseveres under trial; for once he has been approved, he will receive the crown of life which the Lord has promised to those who love Him." Keep in mind that every Christian loves the Lord; we all have an undying love for Him (Ephesians 6:24). So James is telling his readers that we can be encouraged in the midst of trials, knowing that Jesus is our reward.

Imagine persevering through trials and difficulties, and at the end being presented with the crown of life. This crown isn't just a symbol of your endurance, it also represents the very source of life itself, Jesus. John 14:6 says, "I am the way, and the truth, and the life; no one comes to the Father except through Me." Jesus is the crown that awaits those who endure, and through Him, we are more than victorious.

The crown of righteousness also refers to Jesus. As 1 Corinthians 1:30 states,

> But it is due to Him that you are in Christ Jesus, who became to us wisdom from God, and righteousness and sanctification, and redemption.

Christ is our righteousness, and there is no righteousness outside of Him. In 2 Timothy 4:8, we read,

> In the future there is reserved for me the crown of righteousness, which the Lord, the righteous Judge, will award to me on that day; and not only to me, but also to all who have loved His appearing.

Every Christian longs for the return of Christ, so once again, this is about a crown that all saints will share in: Jesus Himself.

Finally, there is the crown of glory. This crown represents the fullness of God's glory. 1 Peter 5:4 says, "And when the Chief Shepherd appears, you will receive the unfading crown of glory." We already have a taste of this glory, but in eternity, we'll fully experience it through Jesus. He is our source of glory, as stated in John 17:22: "The glory which You have given Me I also have given to them, that they may be one, just as We are one."

These crowns represent the very person of Jesus. They are a reminder of who He is to us and what He has done for us.

In Heaven, we will lay these crowns at His feet, declaring that He alone is worthy of all honor and glory. Revelation 4:10–11 says,

> The twenty-four elders will fall down before Him who sits on the throne, and they will worship Him who lives forever and ever, and will cast their crowns before the throne, saying, "Worthy are You, our Lord and our God, to receive glory and honor and power."

So, in the midst of trials and difficulties, remember that there are "crowns" waiting for you. No, these are not rewards for your good works, but reminders of the ultimate reward—Jesus Christ. He is your life, your righteousness, and your glory. Through Him, you are part of a royal priesthood, and you are more than victorious!

Let's Make It a Conversation!

1. How does the concept of crowns in the New Testament differ from the traditional understanding of crowns as rewards for good works?
2. React to this statement: Seeing crowns as rewards for good works is just a form of heavenly materialism.
3. In what ways do the crowns of life, righteousness, and glory represent Jesus and what He means to you?

PART E

FREEDOM

40

How should we view the Law?

Quick Answer

Romans 7:4 tells us that we believers have died to the Law through Jesus Christ so that we can bear fruit for God. Believers are not bound by the 613 laws given to Jews. Even the Apostle Paul described his inability to obey the Law. Galatians 3:10 says the Law is all-or-nothing, and James 2:10 says that breaking one command makes you guilty of breaking all of the Law. The Law is impossible to keep, and that's how it drives us to see our need for God's grace. Salvation in Jesus causes us to die to the Law forever, and God's grace is more than enough to inspire godliness in us.

Diving Deeper

As believers in Jesus Christ, we have been made to die to the Law through His crucifixion. As Romans 7:4 states,

> Therefore, my brothers and sisters, you also were put to death in regard to the Law through the body of Christ, so that you might belong to another, to Him who was raised from the dead, in order that we might bear fruit for God.

Through our spiritual union with Jesus in His death and resurrection, we've been freed from the requirements of the Law. (To be specific, Jewish believers are freed from the Law, but Gentiles were never even invited to the Law. So, the Gentile is freed from the conscience which bears the righteous requirements of the Law—see Romans 2:15.)

The Law is an impossible standard, intended by God to reveal our need for His grace. As Paul says in Romans 7:15, even as a devout Pharisee, he was unable to obey the Law. And as Galatians 3:10 and James 2:10 make clear, anyone who tries to obey the Law is under a curse and guilty of breaking all of it. This means that the Law is not just strict, but impossible to keep. And that's the whole point!

Nobody can get right and stay right with God through the Old Testament Law. This is why salvation in Jesus must be a free gift. By dying to the Law in Him, we're no longer under sin's power. And God's grace is sufficient to inspire godliness within us (2 Corinthians 12:9; Titus 2:11–12).

As Christians, we are not bound by the 613 laws given to the Jews, nor by the Ten Commandments (which include a mandatory Sabbath observance). We have been made to die to the Law through the death of Christ so that we might live to God and bear fruit for Him (Galatians 2:19; Romans 7:4). The Law served to reveal our inability to obtain righteousness through our own efforts and pointed us to the grace of Jesus as the only means of salvation. Now as believers, we bear the fruit of the Spirit, not the "fruit" of the Law. The Holy Spirit is our source for upright living, and He will never lead us to sin.

After salvation, it might seem that the Law, or a set of moral guidelines, would keep us from sinning. But the Bible presents a different perspective. Paul's letter to the Romans delves into the idea that an environment of attempted Law-keeping actually fuels sin (Romans 5:20; Romans 7:8). Self-effort is called upon to keep the Law, and this provides opportunity for sin to then seize control. But by breaking free from the constraints of the Law, we can break free from sin's grip on our lives: "For apart from the Law sin is dead" (Romans 7:8).

As Christians, we are dead to the Law, not under the Law, and Christ is the end of the Law for us who believe (Romans 6:14; 10:4). Jesus's grace is more than enough to empower you to live a godly life. Through your co-crucifixion with Christ, you're given the freedom from the Law forever. Your new identity together with the indwelling Christ provides you with the strength and inspiration needed to overcome sin. His grace is truly enough in every way!

Let's Make It a Conversation!

1. Can you describe how the concepts of "death" and "marriage" are used in Romans 7:4 to describe the experience of salvation?

2. React to this statement: The Law is not a multiple-choice test or a choose-your-own-adventure situation. It's an all-or-nothing proposition!

3. In your opinion, what are some of the factors that make it difficult for people to fully rely on God's grace and not look to Law-based living?

4. React to this statement: Being under the Law leads to more sin, not less.

41

What does it mean that Jesus fulfilled the Law?

Quick Answer

Christ fulfilled the Law through His life and death on the cross (Romans 8:4; Matthew 5:17). The Law acts as a tutor, revealing humanity's sinfulness and the need for a Savior, but once faith in Christ is accepted, it is no longer necessary (Galatians 3:19–23).

The Law is still good and useful for pointing out people's sin and showing them their need for a Savior, but once they're saved, the Law's purpose has been fulfilled. Paul says the Law is for unbelievers (1 Timothy 1:9; Romans 10:4), while believers have been set free from it and are dead to it (Galatians 5:1; Romans 7:4).

Jesus said not one jot or tittle of the Law would pass away (Matthew 5:18). So the Law is not dead, it is fulfilled. It serves a purpose for the unbeliever, but for the believer, it is fulfilled through the person and work of Jesus Christ. Simply put, the Law is not dead, but we believers are dead *to* the Law. Big difference!

Diving Deeper

The Law, as given through Moses, has been fulfilled by Christ in both His life and His death on the cross (Romans 8:4). The entire Law, from the Ten Commandments to the rituals and sacrifices, all pointed to Christ as the ultimate solution for humanity's sin (Matthew 5:17; Romans 10:4). The Law acts as a tutor, revealing the depth of our sinfulness and showing us our need for a Savior. But once we come to faith in Christ, we are no longer under that tutor, for Christ is the end of the Law for believers (Galatians 3:25; Romans 10:4).

Jesus fulfilled the Law for the whole world, but only those who believe in Him receive the benefit of that fulfillment. Unbelievers, whether they are Jews or Gentiles, remain under the condemnation of the Law or under the requirements of the Law written on their conscience. Perhaps you've heard the expression, "My conscience is killing me." This is a reflection of the fact that the Law kills (2 Corinthians 3:6; Romans 2:15).

However, the Law is not bad; it's good and is to be used properly in the life of an unbeliever (1 Timothy 1:8–9; Romans 10:4). The Law points out the depth of humanity's sinfulness so that people see their need for a Savior (Romans 3:19–20; Galatians 3:19–23). But believers have been set free from the Law, and we're dead to it (Galatians 5:1; Romans 7:4). In this way, Jesus has fulfilled the Law for us and in us:

> For what the Law could not do, weak as it was
> through the flesh, God did: sending His own Son in
> the likeness of sinful flesh and as an offering for sin,
> He condemned sin in the flesh, so that the require-
> ment of the Law might be fulfilled in us, who do
> not walk according to the flesh but according to the
> Spirit. (Romans 8:3–4)

Through His life, death, and resurrection, Christ has satisfied the demands of the Law and has set us free from its condemnation. As believers, we are not under the Law but under grace (Romans 6:14). We live in obedience to God, not through our own efforts at Law-keeping, but through the power of the Holy Spirit within us (Galatians 5:16).

Let's Make It a Conversation!

1. React to this true statement: The Law is not dead, but we believers have died to the Law. Big difference!
2. How is the Law a tutor for the unbeliever?
3. React to this false statement: The Law doesn't save us, but we believers still need it for daily living.
4. What does it mean to you personally that Jesus fulfilled the Law?

42
Are Christians bound by the Ten Commandments?

Quick Answer

The Ten Commandments seem to be a holdout for many Christians who recognize that Jesus freed us from the Law yet argue that we're still under the Commandments for daily living. However, being under the moral law (the Ten Commandments) cannot produce godliness. In Romans 7, with "Thou shalt not covet" in mind, the Apostle Paul says we need to live *apart from* the Law (specifically the Ten Commandments) to find real victory over sin. Similarly, in 2 Corinthians 3, the Apostle Paul calls the Ten Commandments a "ministry of condemnation" and a "ministry of death." Through the New Covenant, we participate in a better ministry with more "glory" than the Ten Commandments: the ministry of the indwelling Holy Spirit. The Holy Spirit will never lead us to sin (to lie, to steal, to murder, etc.). God is counseling us toward godliness in all we do, and how we get there is important. Law-keeping is not our source or goal. The indwelling Christ is our source for godly living, and trusting Him is our primary goal in life. This means the fruit of the Holy Spirit is all the daily, upright living we'll ever need!

Diving Deeper

While many recognize that Christians are no longer under the Law, the Ten Commandments appear to be a modern-day "holdout" of sorts. Some argue that even though Jesus freed us from the ceremonial law, we're still under the Ten Commandments for daily living. Ironically, though, most people who claim we're under the Ten Commandments can't even recite them all, much less keep them!

The New Testament makes it clear that the Law exists to reveal the depth of humanity's sin so we can find our Savior (Galatians 5:22–23). Scripture states that the Law is for the unbeliever (1 Timothy 1:9), and it cannot produce godliness. Romans 7:7–8 states this clearly: "But sin, taking opportunity through the commandment, produced in me coveting of every kind; for apart from the Law sin is dead."

It's important to note that "You shall not covet" is one of the Ten Commandments, the moral law. Romans 7 is saying that sin takes its opportunity through the Ten Commandments. Paul is therefore instructing us that we need to live apart from the Law—specifically the Ten Commandments—to find real victory over sin. It's not Jesus-plus-Moses that makes us righteous before God. For believers, it is Jesus plus nothing. And the natural byproduct of knowing Jesus is that we will bear the fruit of God's Spirit (Galatians 5:22–23).

Additionally, Paul's words in 2 Corinthians 3:7–10 call the Ten Commandments a ministry of condemnation and a ministry of death:

> But if the ministry of death, in letters engraved on stones, came with glory so that the sons of Israel could not look intently at the face of Moses because of the glory of his face, fading as it was, how will the ministry of the Spirit fail to be even more with glory? For if the ministry of condemnation has glory, much more does the ministry of righteousness excel in glory. For indeed what had glory in this case has no glory, because of the glory that surpasses it.

Here, the Ten Commandments (the only part of the Law "engraved in letters on stones") are called a ministry of condemnation and death. And throughout the New Testament, Paul makes it clear that we died to the entire Law so that we can now trust the indwelling Christ fully and completely (Galatians 2:19; Romans 7:4). Through the New Covenant, we participate in a ministry with more "glory" than the Ten Commandments: the ministry of God's Spirit. He will never lead us to sin (to lie, to steal, to murder, etc.), as His love "covers a multitude of sins" (1 Peter 4:8). The Holy Spirit is more than powerful enough to produce all the godliness and all the fruit we'll ever need to bear in life!

Let's Make It a Conversation!

1. How do you understand the relationship between the Ten Commandments and the believer?

2. How do you reconcile the idea that the Ten Commandments are a ministry of condemnation and death?

3. How does understanding the context of the commandment against coveting enhance the meaning of the statement "apart from the Law sin is dead" (Romans 7:8)?

4. React to this statement: Those who say we're only free from the sacrificial law trust Jesus for His blood, but not His life in us.

5. Titus 2:11–12 says the grace of God teaches us to live godly lives. What does it look like to trust God's grace alone for daily living?

43

Do Christians need to keep the Sabbath?

Quick Answer

Some Christian teachings encourage observance of the Old Testament Sabbath, which prohibits physical labor from Friday at sundown to Saturday evening. But the Sabbath was designed to reflect God's rest after creating the universe. And the Sabbath was a shadow of spiritual rest available through belief in Jesus Christ. Hebrews 4:3 states that believers have entered God's rest, which is a rest from trying to earn salvation through their own works and a reliance on Christ's work for salvation. The Apostle Paul encouraged Christians not to let anyone judge them for not keeping the Sabbath (Colossians 2:16). Therefore, believers do not need to observe the Old Testament Sabbath, as it is a matter of the Law and has been fulfilled by Jesus Christ.

Diving Deeper

The concept of the Sabbath, or setting aside a day of the week for rest, is rooted in the Old Testament. In Exodus 20:8–11, God commanded the Israelites to observe the Sabbath, the seventh day of the week, as a day of rest, reflecting God's own rest after creation. This commandment was part of the Law given to the Israelites, which also included other commandments such as not stealing, not committing adultery, and not bearing false witness.

However, as the New Testament teaches, the Law was a shadow of things to come, and Jesus Christ is the reality to which it pointed. The Sabbath rest under the Law was a foreshadowing of the spiritual rest available to believers in Jesus Christ. In Hebrews 4:3, it states that believers have entered God's rest, which is defined as a rest from our own efforts to earn salvation and a confidence in the finished work of Jesus Christ.

Christians are dead to the Law, including the Sabbath, as it is through faith in Jesus Christ that we are made right with God and not by any Law-keeping. This is why the Apostle Paul wrote to the Colossians that they should not let anyone judge them for not keeping a Sabbath day (Colossians 2:16).

Sabbath observance is not a requirement, but rather a shadow of the spiritual rest that is found in Jesus Christ. The Sabbath was designed to be a physical reminder of God's rest and provision, but that reminder is fulfilled in Jesus Christ, who Himself is our Sabbath rest. And we can rest in Him every day!

Let's Make It a Conversation!

1. What is your understanding of the biblical teaching around the Sabbath? How has your understanding changed over time (if at all)?

2. How does understanding the Sabbath as a foreshadowing of spiritual rest in Jesus Christ affect your view?

3. Reflect on the implications of the biblical truth that believers have *already* entered into God's rest. How does this affect your daily life and perspective on relationship with God?

44

Is tithing 10 percent of income required for Christians?

Quick Answer

Many teach that tithing—giving 10 percent of one's income—is required to please God, citing Malachi 3:8–10. However, there is no evidence in the New Testament that Christians are required to give a certain percentage. In the Old Testament, tithing was established to support the priests, with an annual average of about 23 percent given. Some cite Abraham's gift to Melchizedek as an argument for tithing, but it was a one-time gift of war spoils and not something for Christians to imitate today. The New Testament letters do not prescribe tithing, and Jesus calls tithing a matter of the Law (Matthew 23:23) which Christians are not under. Christians are free to give from the heart, with no pressure or required percentage (2 Corinthians 9:7).

Diving Deeper

Many churches teach that Christians are robbing God if they do not give a tithe, using Malachi 3:8–10 to argue that believers are required to give 10 percent of their income to God. However, this is not the teaching of the New Testament. There is not one single instance where the apostles instruct New Testament believers to give a certain percentage. Instead, the New Testament invites believers to give freely from the heart, not under any pressure or compulsion.

In the Old Testament, tithing was a practice instituted for the Israelites to support the Levitical priests who were not allowed to earn outside income (Leviticus 27:30–33; Numbers 18:20–24). The tribes of Israel gave from their own income and crops to support the priests, who were serving God in their roles and thus unable to farm or earn income. The amount given was up to 23 percent per year, which is significantly different from the 10 percent mandate commonly promoted today. Note that Jesus came to fulfill the Law, meaning that New Testament believers are *not* under its regulations—and therefore not under tithing.

Some suggest that Abraham's gift to Melchizedek (which preceded the Law) is a good argument for the 10-percent mandate today (Genesis 14:18–20). However, it's important to note that Abraham first went to war, killed people, and took their belongings—giving a tenth (one time) to a king. This was a common practice in the Middle East to convey respect. This one-time giving of spoils of war is not something we are called to imitate today.

The New Testament does not prescribe tithing as a requirement. Jesus explicitly calls tithing a matter of the Law in Matthew 23:23, and Christians are not under the Law (Romans 6:14; Galatians 5:18). Therefore, Christians are not under the tithe.

Some people argue that a tithe is a "starting point" and that we should give more than the Law's requirement, since grace is greater than the Law. But grace is not a new and stricter standard on top of the Law. As New Covenant believers, we don't start with avoiding pork and shellfish and then "graduate" to avoiding other foods on top of those. The Law is not the starting point, and 10 percent is not the starting point for our giving.

Instead of being bound by a specific percentage or practice, New Testament believers are encouraged to give as they truly desire:

> Remember this: Whoever sows sparingly will also reap sparingly, and whoever sows generously will also reap generously. Each of you should give what you have decided in your heart to give, not reluctantly or under compulsion, for God loves a cheerful giver. And God is able to bless you abundantly, so that in all things at all times, having all that you need, you will abound in every good work. (2 Corinthians 9:6-8 NIV)

Clearly, the more we invest in sharing the Gospel message with others, the more spiritual harvest can be reaped. But the Spirit of God will inspire us to give from the heart, without any requirement to tithe. Giving should come from an attitude of gratitude and generosity, not from any compulsion or pressure (2 Corinthians 8:11–14).

In conclusion, the idea that Christians are required to give a 10-percent tithe of their income to please God is not supported by the New Testament. To claim such a thing is to teach the wrong covenant (Old instead of New), the wrong percentage (10 percent instead of 23 percent), and the wrong motivation (pressure instead of joy). Tithing was an Old Testament practice that Jesus fulfilled, and believers are free to give from the heart, without any pressure or compulsion.

Let's Make It a Conversation!

1. What teachings or beliefs have you encountered regarding the practice of tithing? How have these teachings been promoted in your experience?

2. In light of the discussion above, how do you think your perspective on the subject of tithing may have shifted or changed? How might this affect your practice of giving in the future?

3. Reflecting on the idea of giving from the heart rather than under compulsion or pressure, what specific attitudes do you believe would embody this concept for you personally? How might this differ from how you have approached giving in the past?

45

Why do the teachings in the Sermon on the Mount seem impossible?

Quick Answer

The Sermon on the Mount, found in Matthew 5–7, is often seen as a source of inspiration for spiritual growth. But as Jesus delivers this powerful message, He presents a demanding and challenging set of instructions for His audience. He calls for the cutting off of hands and plucking out of eyes and encourages His listeners to be perfect, like God. Furthermore, Jesus equates lust with adultery, and anger with murder. To top it all off, He urges His listeners to resolve conflicts before offering sacrifices and reminds them that they will be held accountable by the Sanhedrin, a Jewish council from two thousand years ago. It's important to keep in mind that the Sermon on the Mount must be understood within the context of Judaism. Jesus is intentionally setting an impossibly high standard (the true spirit of the Law) to reveal the spiritual slavery and hypocrisy of His Jewish audience. So, the Sermon on the Mount is not a warm and fuzzy passage for Christian growth. Instead, it serves as a powerful wake-up call for anyone who thinks they can keep the true standard of the Jewish law.

Diving Deeper

While many look to the Sermon on the Mount as the gold standard for Christian living, Jesus makes it clear that His sermon is actually an expansion on the Law (Matthew 5:19). In the sermon, Jesus tells His audience to cut off their hands and to pluck out their eyes in their fight against sin. In so doing, He is revealing their lack of commitment and the true standard of dedication required to defeat sin in their current state:

> "If your right eye makes you stumble, gouge it out and throw it away. It it is better for you to lose one

part of your body than for your whole body to be thrown into hell. And if your right hand causes you to stumble, cut it off and throw it away. It is better for you to lose one part of your body than for your whole body to go into hell." (Matthew 5:29–30 NIV)

Notice that Jesus also speaks of Hell here, whereas believers are not in danger of Hell. Furthermore, in the Sermon on the Mount, Jesus reveals that looking with lust equals adultery and that anger is equal to murder. He tells His audience that their righteousness must surpass that of the Pharisees and that they must be perfect like God (Matthew 5:48). Interestingly, Jesus also informs His audience that they must get right with others before offering their animal sacrifices on the altar. However, New Testament believers do not offer animal sacrifices on altars. The cross of Christ replaced all altars for us, and there are no altars today.

It's essential to consider the context in which Jesus delivered this sermon. He explicitly states that His teachings are an expansion on the Law, and the standard of obedience He sets is not only difficult but impossible for anyone to meet. Jesus also informs His hearers that if they do not comply with this level of obedience, they'll answer to the Sanhedrin—a Jewish council from two thousand years ago. Once again, believers today have no relationship to the Sanhedrin and are not accountable to them in any way. Clearly, there's a context of Judaism that needs to be considered when interpreting the Sermon on the Mount. Jesus purposely introduces the perfect and impossible standard of the Law in order to expose the hypocrisy of His Jewish audience and their addiction to sin.

In conclusion, the Sermon on the Mount is not a guide for Christian living, but an expansion on the Law. Jesus uses strong language and dire consequences, such as cutting off one's hand or plucking out one's eye if it causes one to sin, and refers to Hell to drive home the point that obedience to the Law is impossible for any human being. He also reveals that true righteousness must surpass that of the Pharisees, and that one must be perfect as God is perfect.

It's important to note that this sermon was delivered to a Jewish audience, and the practices and consequences mentioned—such as offering sacrifices on altars, being accountable to the Sanhedrin, and going to Hell—do not apply to believers today. The Sermon on the Mount serves as a wake-up call to realize that righteousness and victory over sin can only come from God as a free gift, not through human effort. The sermon exposes its audience's hypocrisy and addiction to sin and ultimately highlights their desperate need for God's grace instead.

Let's Make It a Conversation!

1. Why do you think so many people water down the Sermon on the Mount and view it as a sweet, inspirational passage for Christian growth?

2. How does Jesus's use of strong language and dire consequences in the Sermon on the Mount serve to drive home

the point that obedience to the Law is impossible for any human being?

3. How does the Sermon on the Mount serve as a wake-up call to the realization that righteousness and victory over sin can only come from God as a free gift, not through human effort?

46

Why did Jesus emphasize the two greatest commandments?

Quick Answer

People often believe they should try to love God with all their strength and try to love others as they love themselves. However, this belief results from misinterpreting a conversation between Jesus and a Pharisee (Matthew 22:34–40). Here, an expert in the Law came to Jesus and asked Him what were the greatest commands *in the Law*. Jesus answered that the greatest commandments in the Law are to love God with all your strength and to love your neighbor as yourself. But we believers are not under the Law, and there is a better way of loving under the New Covenant. Jesus teaches us a new commandment: to love one another as He loved us. This new commandment takes the pressure off of us to love God perfectly and instead, it focuses on receiving and believing in God's love and transmitting His love to others. Under the New Covenant, we are called to believe in the sheer magnitude of Christ's love for you and then to give it away freely.

Diving Deeper

Jesus taught that the greatest commandment in the Law is to love God with all of your heart, soul, mind, and strength, and to love your neighbor as yourself (Matthew 22:37; Mark 12:30). But as believers in the New Covenant, we have a deeper motivation for loving: the love of God poured within us (Romans 5:5).

When Jesus issued the new commandment to "love one another, even as I have loved you" (John 13:34), He wasn't simply rehashing the old Law. He was providing us with a new way of loving, one that is rooted in the belief and understanding of God's love for us.

Under the Law, the greatest commandment was to love God perfectly and with all your strength, but this is an impossible standard to live up to. However, under the New Covenant, we are called to receive and believe in God's love and to transmit this love to others.

Believing in the sheer magnitude of Christ's love for us and sharing it freely with others makes the call of the Gospel "easy and light" (Matthew 11:28–30). This new way of loving takes the pressure off of us to love perfectly and allows us to simply receive and give love freely. The good news is, it's all made possible by the grace of God.

In conclusion, the old way of trying to love God and others through our own strength and effort is one of bondage and drudgery. It is an impossible task, as we can never truly love perfectly on our own. However, under the New Covenant, we have been given a new way of loving—one rooted in belief and understanding of God's immense love for us. This allows us to receive God's love and reflect it to others, experiencing freedom and joy in the process. Instead of striving to love perfectly, we can simply believe in the magnitude of God's love for us and give it away freely. This is the true essence of the new commandment and the heart of the Gospel message.

Let's Make It a Conversation!

1. How does understanding and believing in God's love for us change the way we love God and others?

2. How is the new commandment of loving one another as Christ loved us different from the "greatest commandment" in the Law to love God with all our heart, soul, mind, and strength?

3. In what ways do you find it hard to love, and how can understanding and believing in the love of God change that? How do you think the freedom and joy of reflecting God's love to others would change your day-to-day life?

47

Is the Old Testament important for believers today?

Quick Answer

The Old Testament is important for New Testament believers, because the entire Bible is the inspired Word of God. Second Timothy 3:16 tells us that *all* Scripture is useful for teaching, rebuking, correcting, and training in righteousness. The Old Testament provides insights on God's creation, humanity's abandonment of Him, and God's pursuit of humanity through His love and mercy. The Psalms and Proverbs offer valuable truths about God's view of wisdom, trust in Him, and much more.

However, it's important to read the Old Testament through the lens of the New Covenant. For example, dietary restrictions listed in Leviticus no longer apply, and every day is now considered holy or set apart in Christ. The New Covenant also brings once-for-all-time forgiveness and the permanent indwelling of the Holy Spirit. Hebrews 11:37–40 states that the Old Testament believers were waiting for something better, which Jesus brought through His death and resurrection. Therefore, the Old Testament should be read, studied, and learned from while understanding that we live in the era of the New Covenant.

Diving Deeper

Second Timothy 3:16 is an important verse that highlights the authority and usefulness of the Bible. At the time this verse was written, only the Old Testament was widely considered Scripture. Paul's statement that "all Scripture is inspired by God" refers specifically to the Old Testament, not just the New Testament letters being written.

The Old Testament is a rich source of wisdom and insight into God's character and purposes. It tells the story of God's creation of the world and humanity and how Israel, God's chosen people, were called to be a light to the nations. Through the Old Testament, we see how humanity strayed from God's ways and how God, in His love and mercy, pursued them. The Psalms, Proverbs, and other writings offer a window into the hearts and minds of those who walked closely with God, and the laws and regulations of the Mosaic Covenant reveal God's perfect—and ultimately impossible—standard.

However, as Christians, we understand that the Old Testament is to be read in the light of the New Covenant that was established through the death of Jesus Christ. The Old Testament laws, such as dietary restrictions and the Sabbath, are not binding on Christians, as they were only shadows of the reality that was fulfilled in Christ. Similarly, the sacrifices and rituals of the Old Testament were done away with by the once-for-all sacrifice of Jesus. Through the New Covenant, we enjoy the indwelling of the Holy Spirit, who was not present in that intimate way within the believer in the Old Testament era.

In light of the New Covenant, we can see that the Old Testament was not an end in itself, but a preparation for the coming of Christ. Hebrews 11:37–40 speaks of the Old Testament believers as having faith in something that was yet to come. It is through Jesus that we now have access to the fullness of God's promises and blessings.

In summary, the Bible as a whole is the inspired Word of God. The Old Testament is of great value as it reveals God's character and purpose, but it should be read, studied, and learned from with the understanding that we're living in the New Covenant era ushered in by the death of Christ.

Let's Make It a Conversation!

1. In reading the Old Testament, what aspect of God's character do you find particularly noteworthy and why?
2. Can you share a favorite Old Testament character or story, and explain why it resonates with you?
3. When studying the Old Testament, have you found yourself interpreting it through the lens of the New Testament? Why or why not?
4. How do your perspectives on the Old Testament change when considering it in the context of the New Covenant? Can you give examples?

48

What is the New Covenant?

Quick Answer

The New Covenant, also known as the New Testament in the Bible, is God's promise of salvation through Jesus Christ's death and resurrection. This covenant fulfills the promises made in the Old Covenant, which was God's agreement with the Israelites. The New Covenant allows for all people to have a personal relationship with God through faith in Jesus Christ. It promises total forgiveness for all sins, a new heart, freedom from Law-based living, and new birth as God's children. It is the gospel of grace inaugurated in the blood of Jesus Christ (Luke 22:20; Hebrews 9:16–17).

Diving Deeper

The New Covenant, as outlined in the Bible, is a promise made by God to save all those who believe in Jesus. This promise encompasses several key elements, including complete forgiveness for sins, the gift of a new heart, freedom from the Law (and the conscience that kills), and new birth as God's children.

The term "covenant" in the New Testament is translated from the Greek word *diatheke*, which means "will" or "testament." This concept is similar to the idea of an earthly will, a legal document by which beneficiaries receive an inheritance upon the death of the testator. In the case of the New Covenant, believers receive a spiritual inheritance through the death of Jesus.

One of the most significant aspects of the New Covenant is the total forgiveness of sins. This is mentioned in Hebrews 8:12 and 10:14, and it is a complete cleansing of all transgressions. Along with forgiveness, the New Covenant also includes the gift of a new heart in which Christ dwells. This is described in Ezekiel 36:26–27 and Hebrews 8:10, and it's a vital aspect of the believer's transformation.

Another important aspect of the New Covenant is freedom from the laws of the Old Testament. This is mentioned in Hebrews 10:10 and Galatians 5:1, and it means believers are not bound by the strict laws and regulations of the Old Covenant. Instead, we're free to live in the love and grace of

God. This is because we have a new heart, a new spirit, and God's Spirit living in us. God's desires are imprinted upon us at the centermost part of our being. Now, we want what God wants!

A final aspect of the New Covenant is new birth as God's children. This is described in 1 John 3:1, Hebrews 8:11, and Galatians 4:6. It means believers are given the rights and privileges of God's children. We are no longer outsiders but are reborn into the family of God, and we all intuitively know God at a heart level (Hebrews 8:11).

In summary, the New Covenant is God's promise to save all who believe in Jesus. It includes total forgiveness of sins, a new heart, freedom from the Law (for Gentiles, the conscience that kills), and new birth as God's children. It's a covenant built on God's oath to remain faithful to Himself forever, and believers are the direct beneficiaries. It's not a promise we make to God, but one that God made to Himself. This promise is based on "two unchangeable things"—God and God—securing our salvation with "an anchor for the soul" (Hebrews 6:18–19).

Let's Make It a Conversation!

1. How has your understanding of the New Covenant been enhanced after reading this answer above? How is it different from the Old Covenant?

2. Why do you think the concept of the New Covenant is not discussed very frequently in church settings?

3. How does the idea of inheriting something rather than earning it relate to the New Covenant?

4. Which aspect of the New Covenant resonates with you the most and why?

5. How does the fact that the New Covenant is a promise God made to Himself impact your understanding of your salvation?

49
When did the New Covenant begin?

Quick Answer

The New Covenant began at the death of Jesus Christ, not at His birth (Luke 22:20; Hebrews 9:16). Jesus lived and ministered under the Old Covenant, and some of His teachings exposed the true spirit of the Old Testament Law (Galatians 4:4). The word "testament" or "covenant" stems from the Greek word *diatheke*, meaning "a will." Remember that a death, not a birth, is required to activate a will or testament. The New Covenant did not go into effect until Jesus died, and the cross is the true dividing line of human history. Some of Jesus's teachings before the cross (the Sermon on the Mount, for example) were designed to show people the futility of trying to keep the Law and to prepare them for a new way of grace. The message of God's grace found in the Gospel becomes even clearer when we understand that the cross is the dividing line between the Old Covenant and the New Covenant.

Diving Deeper

Once we have finished reading the Old Testament, we come to the New Testament, which starts in Matthew 1. But did you know that the New Testament era, or New Covenant, does not really begin in Matthew 1? That's right. It's not baby Jesus in a manger that brings in God's new way of grace. The New Covenant didn't begin until thirty-three years later, with the death of Christ (Luke 22:20; Hebrews 9:16).

The word "testament" (or "covenant") is from the Greek word *diatheke*, which means "a will." Referring to the New Covenant, Hebrews 9:17 says, "For a covenant is valid only when people are dead, for it is never in force while the one who made it lives."

Even the Old Covenant did not go into effect without blood:

> Moses took the blood and sprinkled it on the people, and said, "Behold the blood of the covenant, which the LORD has made with you in accordance with all these words." (Exodus 24:8)

For this same reason, at the Last Supper, Jesus told His disciples the New Covenant would be coming through His blood (not His birth): "This cup, which is poured out for you, is the new covenant in My blood" (Luke 22:20).

This means that Jesus's entire earthly ministry was under the Old Covenant (Galatians 4:4). Jesus was born under the

Law, and we draw the dividing line of human history at the cross, not at the manger:

> But when the fullness of the time came, God sent His Son, born of a woman, born under the Law, so that He might redeem those who were under the Law, that we might receive the adoption as sons and daughters. (Galatians 4:4–5)

Both Jesus and His audience lived during the Old Covenant Law. This is why we see so many harsh teachings from Jesus in which impossible standards are taught: cut off your hand, pluck out your eye, be perfect like God (see the Sermon on the Mount in Matthew 5–7 for examples).

Have you ever wondered why Jesus taught that forgiveness was conditioned upon forgiving others first (Matthew 6:12–15)? Or why He said we must be perfect like God (Matthew 5:48)? This was Jesus teaching the perfect standard of the Law so His hearers would see their need for God's grace instead (Galatians 3:19–23).

In summary, Jesus lived and ministered under the Old Covenant (Galatians 4:4–5), and some of His teachings exposed the true spirit of the Old Testament law. This is why we see so many harsh teachings from Jesus in which impossible standards are taught, such as cutting off your hand, plucking out your eye, and being perfect like God. These teachings were intended to show the proud Jews of His day the impossibility of Law-based living and their need for a new way beginning at His death.

Let's Make It a Conversation!

1. How does understanding the New Covenant help you contextualize Jesus's harshest teachings?

2. How do you reconcile the idea that some of Jesus's teachings are not directly applicable to our current context? (Hint: Consider the true dividing line of human history.)

3. What insights can we gain by recognizing that Jesus's teachings had dual purposes (to reveal the spirit of the Law and to introduce the New Covenant to come), and how does this shape our understanding of His message?

4. What are some of the most meaningful aspects of being a believer under the New Covenant for you personally, and how do they impact your daily life and relationship with God?

50

Can too much grace lead to more sinning?

Quick Answer

The idea that an overemphasis on God's grace will lead to more sinning is a misconception. Titus 2 and Romans 6 both state that grace encourages godly living and frees us from the power of sin. God's grace is not something to be feared, but it's to be embraced and relied on in our daily lives. So, we need more grace, not less, if we want to overcome temptation.

Being afraid of too much grace is like being afraid of too much victory over sin (Romans 6:14)!

Diving Deeper

It's a common misconception that an overemphasis on God's grace will lead to more sinning in the Christian life. However, Scripture makes it clear that grace is what encourages godly living. In fact, we need more grace, not less, if we want to overcome temptation. Saying we can have too much grace is like saying we can have too much freedom from sin.

When we dive deeper into the concept of grace, we find that God announces the opposite of this belief. Titus 2:11–12 states that God's grace teaches us to deny ungodliness and worldly desires and to live in a sensible, righteous, and godly manner. Therefore, we should focus on grace more, not less, if we desire to live uprightly.

In Romans 6, Paul affirms that if we sin, grace does increase. But he also reminds us that believers have died to sin, and that through grace we have received a new heart, a new spirit, and God's Spirit living in us. This means we are no longer slaves of sin but are now slaves of righteousness. God's grace has cured us of our predisposition toward sin, and deep down, we don't want to sin anymore. We are now allergic to sin and addicted to Jesus!

Romans 6:14 says, "For sin shall not be master over you, for you are not under law but under grace." This verse makes it clear that when we are under grace, sin no longer holds power over us. God's grace frees us from the power of sin and offers us the power to live a godly life. This is why we always need more grace, not less. Simply put, God's grace is empowering.

This is in contrast to being under the Law, where sin holds power over us and we're unable to overcome it. So, grace acts as an antidote to sin, and the more we understand and rely on God's grace, the more we'll be able to say no to sin and live a godly life (Titus 2:11–12).

In summary, the idea that an overemphasis on grace will lead to more sinning is a misunderstanding of the true nature of grace. Scripture makes it clear that God's grace actually frees us from the power of sin and encourages upright living. Grace is not something to be feared, but something to be embraced fully. God's grace is not just the treatment for sin, it's the cure!

Let's Make It a Conversation!

1. Have you been trusting in God's grace? Can you share an example of a time when trust was difficult or easy for you?
2. In what ways do you agree or disagree with the idea that those who are "new-hearted" and "slaves of righteousness" can live freely under God's grace and that the result will be good?
3. Can you share an experience or an example that illustrates how you believe God's grace has helped shape your understanding of living a godly life? How does this understanding differ from a works-based approach to life?

51

What are the "spiritual disciplines"?

Quick Answer

The term "spiritual disciplines" is not found in the Bible, but we do see the importance of prayer and other spiritual activities. Actions such as Bible study and prayer are not presented as a list of things to do to become more spiritually mature, but rather as a natural outflow of our relationship with God. Thus, they are not "spiritual disciplines," but rather an ongoing conversation between us and God that is motivated by a desire to know His grace even better. Christianity is not a religious system of habits and rules, but a vibrant relationship of dependence on the indwelling Christ. Prayer is simply talking to Dad, and Bible study is like eating good food. We shouldn't be pressured into doing either one!

Diving Deeper

Although the term "spiritual disciplines" is not mentioned in the Bible, the significance of prayer and studying Scripture is mentioned. These actions should not be seen as a checklist for spiritual growth, but rather as an expression of our relationship with God. Christianity is not a set of regulations and disciplines, but a dynamic bond of reliance on the presence of Christ within us. Prayer and Bible study can be carried out from desire, not obligation.

Prayer, for example, is not a "discipline," as though we need to make ourselves talk to God, but rather, it's an ongoing conversation we can have with our Heavenly Father about anything! In Philippians 4:6–7, Paul encourages believers:

> Do not be anxious about anything, but in every-thing by prayer and pleading with thanksgiving let your requests be made known to God. And the peace of God, which surpasses all comprehension, will guard your hearts and minds in Christ Jesus.

This passage highlights that prayer is not a task to be completed, but is instead a way for believers to communicate with God and bring their concerns to Him.

Similarly, Bible study is not a discipline to be practiced to get closer to God. It's a way for believers to deepen their understanding of Him and gain truth and wisdom from Him. In 2 Timothy 3:16–17, Paul writes,

> All Scripture is inspired by God and beneficial for teaching, for rebuke, for correction, for train-ing in righteousness; so that the man or woman of God may be fully capable, equipped for every good work.

This verse highlights that the purpose of studying the Bible is not to check a task off a list, but rather to gain under-standing and to be equipped to live an upright life in depen-dence on Christ.

It's important to note that Paul practiced self-discipline (1 Corinthians 9:27), but he was not referring to spiritual disciplines in that passage. He was simply presenting his body to Christ out of his own desire to do so (Romans 12:1–2). Paul was motivated by God's grace and his desire to not be mastered by sin. This is different from relying on spiritual disciplines for Christian growth.

We're meant to live by the Spirit in all aspects of our lives, including prayer and Bible study (Galatians 5:22–23). We should not rely on disciplines to live a Christian life. This diminishes the work of Christ and turns Christianity into a system of habits and rules rather than a dynamic relationship with the indwelling Christ who inspires us.

In conclusion, while the concept of "spiritual disciplines" is not found in the Bible, the importance of actions such as prayer and study are emphasized throughout Scripture. However, these actions should not be viewed as a list of tasks to complete in order to become more spiritually mature but as a natural outflow of our relationship with God.

Let's Make It a Conversation!

1. Can you share about your personal experience with "spiritual disciplines"?
2. How do we reconcile the idea of "disciplines" with the concept of a grace-filled relationship with God? How does viewing spiritual activities as "disciplines" versus as an expression

of our relationship with God change a person's approach toward them?

3. React to this statement: Prayer is talking to Dad, and Bible study is like eating good food. We shouldn't be pressured into doing either!

NEW IDENTITY, NEW LIFE

52

Why did Jesus rise from the dead?

Quick Answer

The resurrection of Jesus is a game-changer for Christians. It's a defining moment that separates Jesus from all other people and so-called deities. Not only does it prove that He is the Son of God, but it also gives believers the gift of new life in Him and a new identity.

But the resurrection isn't just a one-time event that happened in the past. It has ongoing, life-changing effects for believers. Without the resurrection, our faith is meaningless, and we have no victory over sin. The resurrection transforms us from slaves of sin to slaves of righteousness, freeing us from the power of death and the grip of Satan.

And the good news doesn't stop there! The resurrection also gives us hope for the future. It assures us that we have been spiritually reborn and also that we will receive new resurrection bodies, just like Jesus did. The resurrection is something to get excited about, so let's celebrate all it means for us as believers.

Diving Deeper

The resurrection of Jesus Christ is the cornerstone of Christianity. As the Apostle Paul declares, "And if Christ has not been raised, your faith is worthless; you are still in your sins" (1 Corinthians 15:17). The resurrection is a powerful testament to the divinity of Jesus, showing that He has the power to conquer sin and death. But the resurrection is also vital for believers, as it is through His resurrection that we're given new life and a new identity in Jesus. As Paul says, "you have been raised with Christ" (Colossians 3:1).

If Jesus had not been resurrected, it would mean that He was just another religious teacher, and His claims of being the source of resurrection life and eternal life would be proven false. But the resurrection demonstrates that Jesus is the Son of God and the embodiment of resurrection life: "I am the resurrection and the life" (John 11:25).

Furthermore, the resurrection is what allows us to be transformed from slaves of sin to slaves of righteousness, as we are "dead to sin, but alive to God in Christ Jesus" (Romans 6:11). It's also what gives us the hope of being raised with new resurrection bodies; as Paul says, what "is sown a perishable body" is "raised an imperishable body" (1 Corinthians 15:42). And it's through the resurrection that we are set free from the fear of death, which Satan had used to hold us captive (Hebrews 2:14–15). As Paul wrote, "The last enemy that will be abolished is death" (1 Corinthians 15:26).

So the resurrection of Jesus is not only proof of His divinity, but it's also a crucial part of what it means for you to be a believer. It's through His resurrection that you are given new life and a new identity, and it's because of His resurrection that you can eagerly await your resurrection body.

Let's Make It a Conversation!

1. In what ways does the resurrection of Jesus Christ demonstrate His identity as the Son of God? How does the resurrection prove Jesus's claims about Himself and His teachings?

2. How does the resurrection of Jesus impact your identity as a believer? In what ways has it given you new life?

3. How does the resurrection of Jesus affect your relationship with God? How does it give you hope and a sense of purpose in this life and the next?

53

Are Christians both saints and sinners?

Quick Answer

Christians are not sinners by nature, but saints. In fact, the New Testament never refers to God's children as sinners. Instead, we are called "saints" (Romans 1:7). This is not just a spiritual identity, but a reality. When we believe in Jesus, we are born again and made righteous, and we possess a new and living heart. We are crucified, buried, and raised with Christ to newness of life and seated with Christ at God's right hand. We are set apart for Him forever (1 Peter 2:9). Paul did refer to himself once as the "chief" of sinners, but that was in reference to his life before conversion when he was persecuting the Church. We may still sin, but we are not defined by our sins.

We are defined by what Jesus did for us and to us through His death and resurrection. We are not sinners anymore. We are saints who sometimes sin.

Diving Deeper

The New Testament paints a powerful picture of who we are as Christians. We are not just sinners saved by grace; we are saints, transformed by the power of God through Jesus Christ.

Think about it: when we believe in Jesus, we are born again (John 3:6), made as righteous as God (2 Corinthians 5:21), and given the divine nature (2 Peter 1:3–4). It's like a complete spiritual heart transplant! We possess a new and living heart (Ezekiel 36:26–27; Hebrews 8:10; Romans 6:17) that allows us to experience the fullness of life in Christ.

At salvation, we're not just forgiven of our sins, but we're crucified, buried, and raised with Christ to a newness of life (Romans 6:4; Colossians 2:12). And as if that weren't enough, we're seated with Christ at God's right hand (Ephesians 2:6). Can you even imagine the honor and privilege of being seated at the right hand of God? Well, you don't have to imagine, because you're actually there!

Some point to 1 Timothy 1:15 to argue that Christians are referred to as sinners in the New Testament. But here, Paul only referred to himself as the "worst of sinners" (NIV) in this passage because of his history of persecuting the Church (Galatians 1:13). He was referring to his condition before salvation.

Like Jack Nicklaus, still considered one of the greatest golfers of all time, Paul felt that he set a record for being the worst sinner of all time. But after his encounter with Jesus on the road to Damascus, he became a transformed man—a saint—and a leader of the people he once persecuted. He was saying that if God could save him, He can save anyone! No sin is too great for God's grace. Your sins are small, and your God is big. And He has qualified you as a saint.

Of course, you still sin, but sin doesn't define you. You are defined by what Jesus did through His death and resurrection. You are no longer a sinner. You're a saint who sometimes sins. You're a child of God, set apart for His glory and purpose forever (1 Peter 2:9)!

Let's Make It a Conversation!

1. How does understanding that Christians are saints rather than sinners change your perception of yourself?
2. In what ways do you still struggle with seeing yourself as a sinner?
3. How might recognizing yourself as a saint affect your daily life choices?

54
What does it mean to be righteous?

Quick Answer

Righteousness, in a biblical context, is to be right with God at the core of your being. It means that on a scale of 1–10, you're an 11! No human is righteous through their own efforts (Romans 3:19–20). But through Christ, we have been imputed and imparted the very righteousness of God (2 Corinthians 5:21; Galatians 3:21; Romans 4:25; Romans 6:18).

Diving Deeper

Through faith in Jesus Christ, we've been given the gift of imputed and imparted righteousness—the very righteousness God Himself shared with us (2 Corinthians 5:21; Galatians 3:21; Romans 4:25; Romans 6:18).

When we believe in Jesus, we're not just given a legal declaration of innocence but an actual impartation of God's righteousness. We're given the righteousness of God Himself. That means we're not just forgiven, we're also infused with God's righteousness at the very core of our being. We're made new and given a new heart and nature (2 Peter 1:3–4; Ezekiel 36:26–27; Hebrews 8:8–12).

This is not just some abstract concept, it's a reality. Paul tells us in 2 Corinthians 5:21 that we have become the righteousness of God. That's who we are now, by nature. This means that we have an "imparted life" type of righteousness (see Galatians 3:21). This is precisely why Romans 4:25 says Jesus was "raised because of our justification." It is the resurrection of Christ (and our co-resurrection in Him) that makes us new and righteous.

When we believe in Jesus, we become slaves of righteousness (Romans 6:18), and we're connected to Christ. We're allergic to sin and addicted to Jesus. As we bear the fruit of His Spirit, we find true fulfillment in living in a manner that is worthy of our calling. This transformation is a change from our previous state of being enslaved to sin to a new state of being obedient from the heart and possessing an undying love for Jesus.

This righteousness empowers you to live a godly life. You now desire what God desires, and you long to live in a way that is pleasing to Him. Because you've been co-resurrected with Christ (Romans 4:25), you've been gifted with Christ's resurrection power to overcome sin and live a victorious life. This means righteousness is your new normal, and sin is unnatural for you.

So, are you ready to experience the reality of imparted righteousness? Believe that Jesus Christ has actually made you like Him at the core, and experience the freedom and empowerment that comes from being *really* righteous!

Let's Make It a Conversation!

1. In your personal experience, is the concept of being as righteous as Jesus easy or difficult to accept? Why?

2. React to this statement: Christians are allergic to sin and addicted to Jesus.

3. Have you ever heard the phrase "slave of righteousness" used before? If so, what was your understanding of it? How does this concept fit into your view of yourself?

4. How do you feel about the idea that as a Christian, righteousness is your new normal and sin is unnatural for you?

55

What does it mean to be united with Christ?

Quick Answer

Salvation is not just about God forgiving our sins, it's also about being placed in union with Christ. When we believe in Jesus, the Holy Spirit comes to live inside us—performing a miraculous surgery on us, removing our old, dead spirit, and giving us a brand-new, righteous spirit that is united with Him. This means the very presence of God is within us, and we are forever "one spirit with Him" (1 Corinthians 6:17). Additionally, our seating with Christ reveals just how close to God we are, and it gives us great confidence in our relationship with God. Jesus's prayer in John 17 was for us to be united with Him and with the Father. It's through this union that we're saved, live our lives, and are assured of God's never-ending love.

Diving Deeper

Christianity is often presented as being primarily about God forgiving our sins. But the Bible teaches there's a second part of the Gospel: our union with Christ. When we believe in Jesus, the Holy Spirit comes to live inside us (Ephesians 1:13). This is an incredible truth, and it means that the very presence of God is within us. The Holy Spirit performs a miraculous surgery on us, removing our old, dead spirit and giving us a brand-new, righteous spirit that's in union with Jesus. This is why we are forever "one spirit with Him" (1 Corinthians 6:17).

Hebrews 13:5 states, "I will never desert you, nor will I ever abandon you." This means that wherever we go, Christ goes with us, and He will never leave us. This is a great comfort to believers, as it means we never have to go through anything alone. Jesus is always with us and in us!

This union with the Spirit also acts as a constant reminder of our identity in Christ. Scripture says the Holy Spirit "testifies with our spirit that we are children of God" (Romans 8:16–17). So, our spirit is in constant communication with God, and He reminds us of our identity as His children. This is why Romans says we've received a spirit of adoption (Romans 8:15). This constant reminder of our identity in Christ helps us to understand who we are and how much He loves us.

Our seating with Christ also reveals just how close to God we are. Too often, religious teachers speak of a proverbial ladder we must climb to get to God. But Ephesians 2:6 reveals that we are already at the top of the ladder! We can't get closer to God than being united with Christ and seated with Him at God's right hand (Hebrews 10:12). This is a profound truth that can give us great confidence in our relationship with God.

In John 17, Jesus prays for all believers to be one with each other and with the Trinity (John 17:21). First, He requests that we would be in the Father and in Him. Second, He asks that the Father give us the glory that He has been given (John 17:20–23). Finally, Jesus prays that we be given the very same love that the Father has for the Son (John 17:26). This is an incredible prayer, and it shows the depth of Jesus's love for us.

As we can see, Jesus prayed for a lot when He was thinking about us. Each of these requests ultimately come from His desire for His children to be united with Him. Our union with Christ is the foundation of our faith, and it is through this union that we are saved, live our lives, and are assured of God's constant presence. It's also through this union that we're given a glimpse into eternity and the boundless nature of God's love. May we always remember and be grateful for the free gift of our perfect closeness with Christ!

Let's Make It a Conversation!

1. How would you explain the concept of being in union with Christ? What does it mean to you personally?
2. How does our union with Christ affect our understanding of what salvation really is? What implications does it have for our understanding of closeness to God?
3. Can you discuss the idea of being "seated with Christ" and what that means to you?
4. How does the idea of Jesus praying specifically for you make you feel? How does it impact your understanding of your relationship with God?

56

Do you need to "die to self"?

Quick Answer

You can be yourself and express Jesus at the same time! It's not about constantly striving to "die to self," but understanding that our old self has *already* died and we've been resurrected as new selves in Christ. This concept is found throughout the New Testament, with Romans 6:6, Galatians 2:20, and Colossians 3:1 all emphasizing our new identity in Him. Instead of constantly battling ourselves, we should focus on counting ourselves alive to God, as stated in Romans 6:11. The statement "I die daily" in 1 Corinthians 15:31, often associated with the idea of "dying to self," actually refers to the physical dangers Paul encountered in sharing the Gospel. So embrace who you are in Christ and *be yourself.* Don't try to kill off what God has called new!

Diving Deeper

Believers often hear the phrase "die to self" when it comes to living the Christian life. However, it's important to note that this phrase doesn't actually appear in the New Testament. Instead, Scripture teaches that our old self has already died—past tense—and we have been raised with Christ as new selves in Him (Romans 6:6; Galatians 2:20; Colossians 3:1). This means that as a believer, you don't need to "die to self" because you're already the new self!

Some may argue that believers need to "die to self" every day in order to live a successful Christian life. However, this implies that the believer's "self" is sinful, which goes against what Scripture says. We are the new self (Colossians 3:10), and we are not fighting a war against ourselves. Jesus said that a kingdom divided against itself cannot stand (Matthew 12:25). As believers, we are not a kingdom divided against ourselves.

How does this square with Luke 9:23 which says a man must "deny himself, take up his cross *daily*, and follow Me"? Actually, the word "daily" does not appear in Luke 9:23 in many early manuscripts. Notably, the *Codex Sinaiticus*, one of the oldest and most complete copies of the New Testament, omits the word "daily" in Luke 9:23. Furthermore, the word "daily" does not appear in either of the other Gospel accounts of the same teaching—Matthew 16:24 and Mark 8:34. Some scholars believe the word "daily" was added later to Luke 9:23 to harmonize with 1 Corinthians 15:31, in which Paul stated, "I die daily." But the context of this passage reveals Paul was referring to the *physical* dangers he encountered while sharing the Gospel message. He was simply stating that he risked his life every day to get the Gospel message out. Paul's words in 1 Corinthians 15:31 have nothing to do with trying to kill off some spiritual part of himself.

In summary, as a believer, you don't need to "die to self." At salvation, you took up your cross and followed Jesus Christ into death. You denied your old self and that old way of living. You asked to be raised to newness of life. And God has done all of that for you! So now you are called to count yourself dead to sin and alive to God (Romans 6:11).

Remember: You're not an obstacle to God. You're His instrument! This means you can learn who you really are and be yourself. You shouldn't try to eradicate what God wants to celebrate!

Let's Make It a Conversation!

1. How has the concept of "dying to self" been portrayed or explained to you? In what ways have you tried to live out this idea?

2. How does the idea of not needing to "die to self" because you're already the new self align or conflict with your previous understanding of this concept?

3. Can you think of specific examples or ways in which you can express your unique personality and display Jesus at the same time?

4. Why do you think many Christians tend to view their "self" as a sinful concept? How does this perspective detract from the full message of our identity in Christ?

57

Why did Jesus tell us to deny ourselves?

Quick Answer

Jesus never intended for believers to deny themselves. After all, we are the new self, and we don't need to deny anything about who we are! What Jesus taught in Matthew was that, at salvation, we're renouncing our old life and choosing new life in Him. At salvation, we're spiritually crucified with Christ and raised to newness of life. Once we're the new self, we can embrace our self, not seek to deny our self. So, if you're in Christ, you've already taken up your cross when you believed in Jesus. Now you can count yourself alive to God and enjoy the new life you have in Him (Romans 6:11). Our fight as believers is against the flesh (the old way to think and the worldly way to walk) and the power of sin, not against our own selves.

Diving Deeper

Are you tired of feeling bad for not denying yourself enough? Do you feel like you can never measure up to the standard of constantly putting yourself last? Well, the Bible actually has a very different message for you.

Yes, some Christian teachings suggest believers need to deny themselves as if their "self" is bad. However, this is not the message of Scripture for the born-again believer. In Matthew 16:24–26, Jesus states that if anyone wants to follow Him, they must deny themselves and carry their cross. But this is not an ongoing denial of self after salvation. It is a one-time decision to deny our old self (in Adam) and become a new self (in Christ).

When we call upon the Lord to be saved, we are renouncing our old life in Adam and seeking new spiritual life in Christ. When we trust in Jesus for salvation, our old self is spiritually crucified with Christ and buried (Galatians 2:20; Romans 6:6). We are then raised with Christ to newness of life (Colossians 2:12). This is what Jesus meant by carrying our cross and denying ourselves. It is not an ongoing act, but rather a one-time crucifixion and resurrection that occurs at salvation.

Contrary to popular religious thought, "self" is not a dirty word for the believer. When we believe in Jesus, "self" becomes a beautiful word, because we are the new self (2 Corinthians 5:17; Colossians 3:10). God doesn't want us to deny our new selves, He wants us to be ourselves!

It's important to note that the word "daily" in Luke 9:23 is not present in the earliest manuscripts and may have been added later by a scribe. The Bible is not teaching that we need to die to ourselves daily, but rather that we've already died with Christ at salvation. When it comes to "daily," now we should daily count ourselves alive to God (Romans 6:11).

In short, every believer has already denied their old self, taken up their cross, died with Christ, and been raised to new life in Him. Yes, there is the ongoing process of the renewing of our minds (Romans 12:2), and this results in transformation over time in our thinking and our actions. But there is no reason to try to "kill" the self that God has made new. So, if you're a believer, learn who you are in Christ as a sin-hating, righteousness-loving child of God. Then, don't deny yourself—be yourself!

Let's Make It a Conversation!

1. Have you ever felt you should deny yourself to become a better Christian? How did it work?
2. React to this statement: Self is not a dirty word if you're the new self.
3. React to this statement: Don't deny yourself. Learn who you are in Christ, and be yourself!

4. React to this statement: There's no longer a cross to carry but a resurrection life to be lived.

58
Should life be "more of God, less of you"?

Quick Answer

Many Christians believe they must "decrease" for Jesus to "increase" in their lives, but this is not what John the Baptist meant in John 3:30. He was referring to the end of his own ministry, not the believer's spiritual journey. As believers, we're united with Christ and made righteous in Him. Our spiritual desires are now *compatible* with God's, and we don't need to decrease for Jesus to increase in our lives. You can fully express Jesus while being yourself. You're not an obstacle to God. You're His instrument!

Diving Deeper

Many Christians believe they must "decrease" in order for Jesus to "increase" in their lives. They may think their own desires get in the way of God's plans, but this understanding misapplies John the Baptist's statement in John 3:30, "He must increase, but I must decrease." This verse is often taken out of context and applied to the believer's spiritual journey, but it is actually referring to John the Baptist's ministry.

John the Baptist was a prophet sent to prepare the way for Jesus, and as Jesus's ministry began to flourish, John knew that his own ministry was coming to a close. He was not saying that his own spiritual self needed to be lessened or eradicated, but rather that his role in the bigger picture of God's plan was coming to an end. Simply put, it was time for Jesus's ministry to take center stage. Therefore, John's statement is not about the believer's spiritual journey but about a specific task that was given to John.

We as believers are united with Christ. As 2 Corinthians 5:21 says, we've been made righteous in Him. This means our desires are now compatible with God's desires and purposes, and we do not need to decrease in order for Jesus to increase in our lives. We can be ourselves, fully expressing Jesus at the same time, without any conflict. This is the vine-branches relationship that Jesus prayed we would enjoy in John 17:13–26.

In Colossians 1:27, Paul tells us that we have been given the mystery of Christ in us, the hope of glory. The Greek word for "mystery" here means a secret or hidden truth that has now been revealed. This hidden truth is that we're united with Christ in a way that means we can live in Him and express Him in our everyday lives.

In conclusion, John the Baptist's statement in John 3:30 is not a call for believers to decrease in order for Jesus to increase, but rather a statement about the end of John's own ministry. We as believers are united with Christ and made righteous in Him, and our desires and actions are now compatible with God's desires and purposes. We do not need to decrease in order for Jesus to increase in our lives. We are not obstacles to God, but rather His instruments. Even more, we are His children and perfectly compatible with Him!

Let's Make It a Conversation!

1. Have you ever struggled with the idea that you must decrease for Jesus to increase in your life? Can you share a specific example of this belief playing out in your journey?

2. How does understanding the context of John 3:30 change your perspective on the statement, "He must increase, but I must decrease"?

3. React to this statement: You're not an obstacle to God. You're His instrument.

59

Is your heart "desperately wicked"?

Quick Answer

Some teach that a believer has a wicked heart (Jeremiah 17:9). However, this is not scriptural. A Christian has a new, righteous, and obedient heart (Ezekiel 36:26–27; Hebrews 8:10; Romans 6:17). Jeremiah 17:9 describes an unbeliever who has not been born again. In contrast, every believer has a new heart, a new spirit, and God's Spirit. And you can trust your new spiritual heart where Christ lives within you. God has cleaned house and moved in!

Diving Deeper

Many believe that Christians are still plagued by a wicked heart, but this is not true according to Scripture. The Bible teaches that every believer has been given a new, righteous, and obedient heart (Romans 6:17). This new heart is a gift from God, given to us at the moment of salvation.

Jeremiah 17:9, which is often cited as evidence, was written long before the New Covenant was established through the death of Jesus Christ. These words refer to the condition of humanity before the born-again experience, not to the hearts of believers today.

As believers, we have been given a new heart, a new spirit, and the indwelling of the Holy Spirit. This new heart is forever obedient to God and is the dwelling place of Christ (Ephesians 3:17). It is a heart that wants to love and obey God.

It's important to remember that we still live in a fallen world, and we will still struggle with sinful thoughts and temptations. However, these sinful desires do not originate from our new heart but from the power of sin that can still wage war against us (Romans 7:17, 20).

Think of computer hardware versus software. You might have a shiny new computer that you just purchased, but it still may need software updates. Likewise, at salvation we receive shiny new "heartware," but we still need software updates (the renewing of the mind). The stinking thinking emanates from our old mindsets, not from our hearts.

God is always working to renew our minds, helping us to understand and live out the reality of our new heart. We can trust that our new desires align with God's desires for us and that through the power of the Holy Spirit, we are able to live uprightly. When we do, we are so fulfilled because we are forever "allergic" to sin and "addicted" to Jesus!

Let's Make It a Conversation!

1. Have you ever struggled with the belief that you have a wicked heart? How has this affected your relationship with God and others? How has your understanding of the new heart given to you at salvation changed this belief?

2. How does considering the difference between the heart of an unbeliever and a believer (before and after salvation) impact your understanding of your own heart and the ongoing struggle with sin?

3. React to this statement: "At the core of your being, you don't really want to sin." How does this align with your personal experiences and understanding of your own heart? Do you think setting your mind on this truth could help you resist temptation better?

60

What's the difference between spirit and soul?

Quick Answer

There is a difference between the soul and the spirit. The spirit (Greek: *pneuma*) is the innermost part of the person, the part that is one with the Lord and made new at salvation. In contrast, the soul (Greek: *psuché*) is the psychology (mind, will, and emotions) of a person. The soul is like a mirror which can reflect the Spirit of God or the power of sin in any moment, depending on our decisions. However, no matter what, the believer's soul is Heaven-ready in any moment if the Lord returns, and their human spirit is the true determiner of spiritual nature and identity. We should not base our understanding of truth on the fluctuations of our emotions (in the soul), but instead look to the deeper place of our human spirit to know who we are in Christ.

Diving Deeper

As believers in Jesus Christ, it's important to understand the difference between the soul and the spirit. The spirit, or *pneuma* in Greek, is the innermost part of a person and is the part that is transformed at salvation. This is the part of us that is one with the Lord (1 Corinthians 6:17). On the other hand, the soul, or *psuché* in Greek, is the psychology of a person, including the mind, will, and emotions.

The soul can be compared to a mirror, reflecting either the Spirit of God or the power of sin, depending on our decisions. However, it's important to note that the believer's soul is *always* Heaven-ready, regardless of the fluctuations of our emotions. It's the spirit and the soul that go to Heaven and are joined to a new resurrection body.

In 1 Thessalonians 5:23, we are told that humans are made up of body, soul, and spirit. The body is the physical "shell" of the person and how we relate to the physical world. This body will eventually grow older and decay, but in Heaven, we will be given new, glorified bodies. The soul, as mentioned before, is the psychology of a person and is involved in a process of learning and growing. However, it is not getting more righteous over time. The spirit, as previously discussed, is the part that is made new at salvation and gives us our spiritual nature. It is the spirit that is replaced at the moment of salvation (Ezekiel 36:26–27). It is the human spirit that has been crucified, buried, and raised with Christ (Galatians 2:20; Romans 6:4; Colossians 2:12).

It's important to not have a "theology of the soul" or base our understanding of truth on the fluctuations of our emotions. We must look deeper to our human spirit to know who we truly are in Christ. This way, we can allow our soul and body to reflect our true spiritual nature and identity. In conclusion, the soul and spirit are distinct parts of our being, with the spirit determining our spiritual identity and the soul reflecting it. Lastly, keep in mind that all parts of us are holy and acceptable to God—even our bodies. So there is no part of you that is rejected by God. He accepts every ounce of you in every way!

Let's Make It a Conversation!

1. How does understanding the distinction between the spirit and soul impact our understanding of our identity?

2. How does the idea that our soul is always "Heaven-ready," regardless of our growth in attitudes or actions, make you feel?

3. Can you explain the concept of basing one's understanding on truth versus emotions in your own words? How can we ensure we're not basing our understanding on emotions?

61

How do you abide in Christ?

Quick Answer

Christians always abide in Christ and don't have to make daily decisions to try to abide in Christ. The Apostle John gives three indicators that believers abide in Christ: He writes that if we have believed the Gospel, and if the Holy Spirit lives within us, and if we know God, then we do abide in Christ (1 John 2:24, 27; 3:6, 9). Jesus's command to abide in Him was an invitation prior to His death and resurrection and prior to Pentecost. Therefore, it would not be until Pentecost that His disciples would be born again, receive power from on high, and truly live (abide) in Jesus Christ forever. Christians sometimes use the word "abide" in devotional contexts where they really mean to convey the idea of choosing to trust God in a situation. But the Bible itself teaches that abiding (living) in Christ is a permanent state for Christians, not something to be done daily.

Diving Deeper

The idea that Christians must make daily decisions to try to abide in Christ is not supported by Scripture. Instead, the Bible is clear that believers always abide in Christ (1 John 2:24; 2:27; 3:6, 9). The Apostle John gives three indicators that we believers do abide (live) in Christ: if we have believed the Gospel, and if the Holy Spirit lives within us, and if we know God, then we do abide in Christ (1 John 2:24, 27; 3:6, 9).

The passage often quoted to support the idea of making daily decisions to abide in Christ is John 15:5: "I am the vine, you are the branches; the one who remains in Me, and I in him bears much fruit, for apart from Me you can do nothing." Here, Jesus is not prescribing an action for Christians to take daily in this passage. Instead, He is simply inviting the Jews of His day to live in Him. He is stressing the importance of spiritual union with Him, because apart from that saving union, they "can do nothing." Notice there are only two possible states—abiding in Him or being apart from Him. This describes a believer who can bear fruit versus an unbeliever who cannot.

Jesus's command to abide in Him (John 15:4) was an invitation prior to His death, burial, and resurrection, and prior to Pentecost. It would not be until Pentecost that His disciples would be born again, receive power from on high, and truly live ("abide") in Jesus Christ forever. Essentially, Jesus's instruction to abide in Him was an evangelistic appeal. Every believer responded to that appeal at salvation, so now we abide in Christ permanently.

To abide simply means "to live." While some Christians use the word "abide" loosely to express the devotional idea of choosing to trust God in a particular situation, the term "abide" (live) in Scripture is actually a permanent state. It's not something that needs to be done on a daily basis. Just as a person doesn't wake up every morning and try to live in their home, Christians should not wake up every morning and try to live in Christ. We permanently abide in Christ, just as He permanently abides in us (John 17:21).

Let's Make It a Conversation!

1. Reflect on this statement: As believers, we are constantly learning and growing, but Christ always abides in us, and we always abide in Him.

2. Have you ever been taught that "abiding in Christ" is something that needs to be actively worked on or decided upon daily? Share your personal experience and understanding of this concept.

3. How does understanding the meaning of "abide" as "to live" change your perspective on this concept?

4. React to this statement: Christ is not trying to abide (live) in you. Likewise, you don't need to try to abide (live) in Him!

62

Are we "followers" of Jesus?

Quick Answer

As a Christian, you can see yourself not just as a "follower" of Jesus, but as one united with Him in spirit. This spiritual union is an ongoing reality. The Holy Spirit guides and empowers you to live in a way that reflects your union with Jesus every moment of your life (1 Corinthians 6:17). You have the opportunity to be led by the Spirit and express the fruit of your union with Jesus in your attitudes and actions (Galatians 5:19–23). This isn't merely about trying to imitate (or "follow") a religious figure from two thousand years ago. It's about recognizing and responding to the indwelling presence of the risen Christ. It's about being led internally at a heart level, not externally through imitating actions.

Diving Deeper

When we think about our relationship with Jesus, the word "follow" often comes to mind. We hear phrases like "following Jesus" or "walking in His footsteps" and it can seem like our entire relationship with Him is based on imitation and external obedience. However, this is not the most accurate way to portray our relationship with Christ. The truth is, as believers, our relationship with Jesus is so much more than just following Him. It involves an intimate spiritual union with Him.

In 1 Corinthians 6:17, Paul tells us that "The one who joins himself to the Lord is one spirit with Him." This means that through our faith in Jesus, we are spiritually bonded or fused to Him forever. We are *one* with Him in spirit. This is a powerful truth that transforms our understanding of what it means to be a Christian. We're not just followers of Jesus, we're united with Him.

This union with Christ is an ongoing reality. Galatians 5:19–23 teaches us that the Holy Spirit leads us internally, guiding and empowering us to live in a way that reflects our union with Jesus. The Holy Spirit is not just an external guide;

He indwells us and leads us from within. This means that every moment of our lives, we have the opportunity to be led by the Spirit and express the fruit of our union with Jesus in our attitudes and actions.

When Jesus told His disciples to follow Him in Mark 8:34, He was inviting them to join Him in His earthly ministry. But today, we live on the other side of the cross under the New Covenant of God's grace. Through the death and resurrection of Jesus, we have been given the opportunity to experience a deeper, more intimate relationship with Him. We're not just "following" Jesus, we're united with Him and led internally by His Spirit.

So, we can recognize His presence within us and learn what to expect from His Spirit. This is not about trying to imitate a religious teacher from two thousand years ago. The truth is that our relationship with Jesus is not just about following Him, it's about being united with Him in spirit. This is a powerful, exciting, and transformative truth. When we truly grasp this truth, we can live with a sense of purpose and joy, knowing we are not merely followers of Jesus. We are united with Christ and inspired from within by the Spirit in every moment of our lives.

Let's Make It a Conversation!

1. How do you believe the concept of "following Jesus" falls short in describing the depth of a Christian's relationship with Him?

2. Can you elaborate on the significance of our union with Christ in relation to daily living?

3. What is your perspective on the idea that it's not about "What *would* Jesus do?" but rather about "What *is* Jesus doing in and through me today?" How does this shift in perspective change the way we approach life?

TEMPTATION AND WARFARE

63

What is "the flesh"?

Quick Answer

When we believe in Jesus, we receive a new identity (and new heart!), which means we don't have to be controlled by old fleshly attitudes. "The flesh" refers to the old sinful habits and mindsets from our pre-believer life. The New Testament encourages us to renew our minds and reject the deeds of the flesh in favor of the thoughts from God's Spirit. The flesh can be both overtly sinful looking or a subtle religious flavor of flesh (an attitude of self-improvement). Believers no longer live in the flesh, as they now live in God's Spirit. By walking by the Spirit, we can choose to think and act in line with who we are in Christ rather than looking back to those old ways of operating. Through Jesus Christ, we enjoy the power to overcome old habits and mindsets and are set free from the power of fleshly attitudes.

Diving Deeper

The flesh (Greek: *sarx*) refers to the old habits, attitudes, and ways of living that were a part of our life before we became believers in Christ. These habits and attitudes can still influence us at times, but as believers, we are no longer ruled by the flesh. Instead, we are given a new heart and identity in Christ (Hebrews 8:10; Ezekiel 36:26–27). In short, we no longer live by the flesh (Romans 8:5, 9), but we can still *walk* by the flesh at times (Galatians 5:19–23).

When we believe in Jesus, God transforms us and gives us a new nature that desires to live uprightly (Romans 8:5, 9). However, the old fleshly attitudes still exist and can cause us to stumble and engage in sinful behavior (Galatians 5:19–23). To overcome this, the Apostle Paul encourages us to continually renew our minds (Romans 12:2) and reject the fleshly attitudes in favor of the counsel from God's Spirit.

A simple way to understand the flesh is to view it as software. When we believe in Christ, we are given new hardware (or "heartware"). God gives us a new heart that desires to live uprightly (Hebrews 8:10; Ezekiel 36:26–27). However, we still have old software running from our former life lived independently of Christ. We have fleshly attitudes and ways of living that have been ingrained into our thinking. These ingrained patterns of thinking are the flesh.

The flesh can take the form of overt sin such as sexual immorality (Galatians 5:19–20), or even a religious, self-improvement type of mindset. The key is to recognize when we're being influenced by the flesh and choose instead to walk by the Spirit (Galatians 5:22–23).

In conclusion, we are no longer slaves to the flesh, but have been transformed into new creations in Christ (2 Corinthians 5:17). It helps to keep in mind that the flesh is *not* the spiritual nature or identity of the believer. The flesh is simply a network of leftover attitudes from our life prior to receiving Christ. We can choose to engage in the deeds of the flesh, but we're no longer compatible with them. And through God's Spirit, we can choose to think and act in line with who we are in Jesus, leaving behind the old mindsets of fleshly (or worldly) thinking.

Let's Make It a Conversation!

1. Can you share your thoughts on the concept of the flesh?
2. In your experience, do you find it more challenging to resist temptations toward immoral, sinful-looking flesh or moral, religious-looking flesh?
3. How do you respond to the idea that as believers, we have a new identity in Christ (new "heartware") but still need a renewing of the mind ("software updates")?

64

Do Christians have a "sinful nature"?

Quick Answer

Christians have a brand-new, righteous self as a result of the resurrection of Christ (2 Peter 1:4; Colossians 3:1; Romans 6:18). This means that, even though we still sin, we're no longer sinful by nature at our core. The Bible does not teach that Christians have a sinful nature, but rather that we're slaves to righteousness. The idea that Christians have a "sinful nature" comes from a mistranslation of the Greek word *sarx* as "sinful nature" in some versions of the Bible. The more accurate translation is "flesh," which refers to our way of thinking and acting independently of Christ.

Diving Deeper

Before we believed in Christ, we were slaves to sin and spiritually dead (Romans 6:18; Ephesians 2:1). But when we accepted the Gospel, God gifted us with a new, righteous self and a new heart that aligns with His nature (2 Corinthians 5:21; Colossians 3:1). We are no longer slaves to sin, but slaves to righteousness (Romans 6:18).

The idea that Christians have a "sinful nature" stems from a misinterpretation of the Greek word *sarx* as "sinful nature." The mistranslation of *sarx* as "sinful nature" in some versions of the Bible can lead to confusion and a belief that Christians are sinful at their core, when in reality they're not. The more accurate translation is "flesh," which refers to the way of thinking and acting independently of Christ (Galatians 5:19–23). As believers, we are no longer enslaved to this way of thinking and have been set free as slaves of righteousness (2 Corinthians 5:17, 21; Romans 6:18).

In 2008, I brought up the poor translation of *sarx* as "sinful nature" in early editions of the New International Version Bible with my editor at Zondervan (which publishes the NIV Bible). I explained how the poor translation creates confusion concerning the nature of the Christian, and how it gives believers the sense that they're fighting a "civil war" within themselves every day. I submitted feedback to my editor, and he passed it along. To their credit, a few years later, the NIV Committee met numerous times about updates to the NIV

Bible, and when the next release took place, the term "sinful nature" was replaced with "flesh" in most instances. (Later, I found out from the chairman of the NIV Committee that I was not the only one to register a request for that change!)

It's important to note that, while we do still experience the pull of fleshly thinking, the flesh is not our nature, but only a way of thinking and acting. The flesh cannot be improved, but over time, our performance (thinking and actions) does change as we choose to walk by the Spirit and not by the flesh. We're now new-hearted children of God who oppose the flesh (1 John 3:1; Galatians 5:17). We can embrace the truth that sets us free and experience the freedom that comes with understanding that we are no longer slaves of sin but slaves of righteousness.

Let's Make It a Conversation!

1. How does understanding that Christians don't have a "sinful nature" change your perspective on your own spiritual journey? How does this understanding affect your daily decisions and actions?

2. In what ways does the translation of *sarx* as "flesh" instead of "sinful nature" change the way you read and interpret Scripture? How does this impact your understanding of your own spiritual self?

3. How can recognizing that the pull of fleshly thinking is not really you assisting in the process of aligning your actions and thoughts with who you really are?

65

How do you resist the power of sin?

Quick Answer

Sin is not a part of who we are, but a force that tempts us. But, as believers, we have the power to say *no* to sin by recognizing that sinful thoughts do not come from us. At salvation, a spiritual transformation took place in which God crucified our old sinful self and raised us up through Jesus's resurrection, making us dead to sin and alive to God. By recognizing our true identity in Christ, we can now count ourselves dead to the power of sin. So, the next time you face temptation, know that those desires are not yours; they are ideas that war *against* you. Remember your true self and your true desires. When you say *yes* to Jesus, you also say *yes* to who you really are!

Diving Deeper

The power of sin (Greek: *hamartia*) is not a verb but a noun. It refers to the sin principle that entered the world at the Fall of humanity. *Vine's Expository Dictionary of New Testament Words* explains that sin is a personified power (with person-like characteristics) that tempts us. We can think of it as a parasite that operates within us. It works in us, but it's *not* us. Saying *no* to sin is saying *yes* to who we truly are. In a sense, God invites us to reinterpret our entire thought life through an entirely new grid.

We say no to sin by recognizing that sinful thoughts do not come from us, and that sin has no power over us

(Romans 6:11–12). When sinful thoughts or temptations come our way, we can make the conscious decision to count ourselves dead to those thoughts and alive to God. In this way, we express our genuine self (the new self), and we express Jesus at the same time.

Scripture is clear that anyone who has died spiritually has been freed from sin's power (Romans 6:7). This death to sin doesn't occur through rigorous Bible study and adhering to spiritual disciplines. It happens when we believe in Jesus. At salvation, a spiritual surgery takes place. God crucifies our old sinful self with Jesus, buries it, and raises us up through His resurrection (Galatians 2:20; Romans 6:4). Because we are now dead to sin, we are not dominated by its power (Romans 6:2). Essentially, we are "allergic" to sin and "addicted" to Jesus!

Paul encourages believers to consider, reckon, or count themselves dead to sin so that they don't submit to *its* lusts (Romans 6:12). It's important to note that the lusts belong to the power of sin, not to the believer. Sin has its own desires that it seeks to impose upon us.

So, the next time you find yourself facing temptation, you can remember those desires are not your own. They are ideas that actually war against you (1 Peter 2:11). You can make the conscious decision to say *no* to sin and say *yes* to who you truly are.

Let's Make It a Conversation!

1. How familiar were you with the concept of sin as a parasitic force at work within us, separate from our true selves? How does this actually make us more responsible for our choices

rather than less responsible? (Hint: If it's not you, you don't have to give in to it, right?)

2. What challenges have you encountered in resisting sin? How might understanding the root of sinful desires impact your ability to resist them?

3. React to this statement: When we say *no* to sin, we're actually saying *yes* to who we really are.

66

Was Paul's struggle in Romans 7 before or after salvation?

Quick Answer

Romans 7 is a hotly debated passage in the New Testament, with some interpreting it as a description of Paul's struggles as a believer with sin. However, context makes it clear that Paul is referring to his attempts at keeping the Law before his conversion. Paul describes himself as being in bondage to sin, which is an odd statement to make, considering he just stated in Romans 6:7 that "he who has died is freed from sin." He also says this bondage to sin occurred "when the commandment came" (Romans 7:9), which was when he was a devout Pharisee, not when he became a Christian.

Diving Deeper

A close examination of the context and language used in Romans 7 makes it clear that Paul is describing his pre-conversion experience.

First, Paul describes himself as being in bondage to sin in Romans 7:14, which is an odd thing to say considering he just stated in Romans 6:7 that "he who has died is freed from sin." Furthermore, he stated that believers are "slaves of righteousness," not sin.

Second, Paul says this bondage to sin occurred "when the commandment came" (Romans 7:9). This commandment, as Paul states earlier in the passage, refers to the Law. This makes it clear that Paul is describing his life before conversion, when he was a devout Pharisee and the commandments came into his life.

Additionally, Paul's use of the past tense when describing his struggle with sin further supports the idea that he is referring to his pre-conversion experience. He states, "I was once alive apart from the Law" (Romans 7:9), which suggests that he is reflecting on his past experience and not describing a current struggle. Furthermore, Paul's use of the first person throughout the passage suggests that he is describing his personal (past) experience and not making a general statement about the experience of believers.

Furthermore, Paul's use of the Law as the source of his struggle, as well as his statement that "sinful passions" were "aroused" by the Law (Romans 7:5), supports the idea that he is describing his experience as a Pharisee trying to keep the Law and not as a believer struggling with sin. The Law, as Paul explains elsewhere, was given as a means of revealing sin and pointing people to the need for salvation.

Lastly, in verse 24, Paul writes, "Wretched man that I am! Who will set me free from the body of this death?" Then, in the next verse, he thanks God for deliverance. This further supports the idea that Paul is describing his pre-conversion experience in bondage to sin and that the salvation experience is his deliverance.

In conclusion, Romans 7 is not a description of a believer's struggles with sin but rather Paul's description of his pre-conversion experience living under the Law. The context and language used in the passage make it clear that Paul is reflecting on his past experience as a devout Pharisee. In short, Paul is describing the normal Law-based life, not the normal Christ-based life of a believer.

Let's Make It a Conversation!

1. What had you believed about Paul's Romans 7 struggle prior to reading this? Do any of the key points made here give you a reason to reconsider your view?

2. In what ways does Paul's use of language and context in the passage support the idea that he is describing his pre-conversion experience as a devout Pharisee?

3. How does Paul's statement in Romans 7:25, "Thanks be to God through Jesus Christ our Lord!" support the idea that he is describing his pre-conversion experience?

4. How might an understanding of Paul's experience described in Romans 7 as being pre-salvation offer believers more hope concerning victory over sin today?

5. React to this important truth: Romans 7 is the normal Law-centered life but not the normal Christ-centered life.

67

Can a believer be possessed by a demon?

Quick Answer

Christians cannot be possessed by demons. God's protection
and presence mean that Satan cannot touch us (1 John 5:18).
However, Satan can still wage war against our minds through
lies and accusations. It's important for believers to set their
minds on the truths of the Gospel and renew their minds to
God's truth to resist the enemy's schemes.

Diving Deeper

Some popular theology suggests Christians can be possessed by demons, but is this biblical? And to what degree
can Satan afflict believers? The Bible teaches that Satan is
real and actively wages war against believers (1 Peter 5:8), but
it also teaches that believers are protected by God and cannot
be possessed by demons (1 John 5:18).

When we believe in Jesus, God removes our sinful spirit
and gives us a new one (2 Corinthians 5:17; Ezekiel 36:26–27).
He also joins Himself to our new spirit (1 Corinthians 6:17;
Ephesians 1:13). There's no room for Satan to reside within us.
God's presence in us is strong, and He won't share us with a
demon.

Satan's war against believers is an *external* one, a war on
the mind. Satan uses lies and accusations to distract us from
our identity in Christ (John 8:44; Revelation 12:10). These

"flaming arrows" of the evil one come at us, but they're not originating from within us (Ephesians 6:16).

To protect ourselves from these attacks, we can put on the armor of God. This includes the belt of truth, the breastplate of righteousness, the shield of faith, the helmet of salvation, the sword of the Spirit (which is the Word of God), and the feet shod with the preparation of the gospel of peace (Ephesians 6:14–17). By putting on the armor of God, we're setting our minds on the truths of the Gospel and fixing our eyes on Jesus (Ephesians 6:11; Colossians 3:2; Hebrews 12:2). This is what Paul had in mind when he instructed us to be strong in the Lord (Ephesians 6:10).

The renewing of our mind also plays an important role (Romans 12:2). As our minds are renewed to God's truth, we will become more aware of the enemy's lies and choose to reject them.

In summary, while the enemy may seek to attack you with thoughts, you are protected by God and cannot be possessed by a demon. In this way, the enemy is all bark and no bite. And by putting on the armor of God and renewing your mind, you can stand against the enemy's schemes. You don't need to be afraid of the forces of darkness, but you can be aware of their tactics and prepared to resist them. Remember, "greater is He that is in you than he who is in the world" (1 John 4:4).

Let's Make It a Conversation!

1. Have you ever known anyone who was demon-possessed? What was the context?

2. Do you believe a Christian can be demon-possessed? Why or why not?

3. What does the armor of God reveal about the nature of Satan's attacks?

4. React to this statement: Jesus lives in you and won't share you with a demon.

68

What is the "armor of God"?

Quick Answer

The armor of God, as described in Ephesians 6, is not a set of actions we must take, but rather Jesus Christ Himself. Each piece of the armor represents a different aspect of Jesus: the belt of truth represents Jesus as the Truth, the breastplate of righteousness represents Jesus as our righteousness, and so on. By putting on Christ, we put on the armor of God and we're able to stand against the devil's schemes. Jesus is not only our defense, but our offense in spiritual battle. He is our righteousness and our peace. Trusting in Jesus as our armor is the key to weathering spiritual attacks.

Diving Deeper

In Ephesians 6, the "flaming arrows" represent attacks of the enemy intended to harm us spiritually. These attacks can take many forms, such as lies, temptations, doubts, and fears that can cause us to become spiritually distracted. The Apostle Paul is encouraging the Ephesian believers to put on the full armor of God so they can stand against the enemy's tactics and be protected from these flaming arrows.

The armor of God is often understood as a set of prayers or actions that we must carry out to protect ourselves from spiritual attack. However, this interpretation misses the true meaning and purpose of the armor. In reality, the armor of God is not something we do, but rather Someone that we put on—Jesus Christ Himself (Romans 13:14).

The pieces of armor described in Ephesians 6 can all be understood as different aspects of Jesus Christ and His work in our lives. The belt of truth represents Jesus as the Truth; the breastplate of righteousness represents Jesus as our righteousness; the shield of faith represents our faith in Jesus; the feet shod with the gospel of peace represent Jesus as the Prince of Peace; the helmet of salvation represents Jesus as our salvation; and the sword of the Spirit represents Jesus as the living Word of God.

In short, putting on the armor of God is the same as putting on Christ. In Colossians 3:14, Paul says, "put on love," and in Romans 13:14 he says, "put on the Lord Jesus Christ." When we look to Jesus Christ as our spiritual protection, we're putting on the armor of God. This is the key to weathering the spiritual attacks from the enemy—trust in Christ, who lives in us. This is why Paul says in Ephesians 6:11, "Put on the full armor of God, so that you will be able to stand firm against the schemes of the devil."

Let's Make It a Conversation!

1. How do you see spiritual warfare playing out in your own life? Have you had any experiences when you felt like you were engaging in spiritual warfare? How did you respond to it?

2. What is your perspective on the armor of God described in Ephesians 6? How does it relate to your understanding of spiritual warfare?

3. How does the truth that the armor of God is Jesus Himself clarify how to protect yourself from spiritual attacks?

4. Of the different pieces of armor described in Ephesians 6, which one do you find most meaningful to you? Why does it resonate with you? What are some ways you "put it on"?

RELATIONSHIP WITH GOD

69

What role does obedience play in the Christian life?

Quick Answer

Many have created a friction between the concepts of grace and obedience. However, grace and obedience are related and beautifully compatible—one flows from the other. Romans 6:17 states that we believers have become "obedient from the heart." By grace, we have been gifted with a new, righteous heart that is obedient to God. This is why we can afford to live under grace and watch as God grows us up as obedient children in His family.

Diving Deeper

Grace and obedience are not mutually exclusive, as some may believe. Instead, they are intimately connected. Romans 6:17 says we have become "obedient from the heart" through God's grace. We have been given new hearts that want what God wants. So our obedience is not based on some heroic effort we drum up, but rather it's a natural response to the obedient hearts we received at salvation.

In John 14:15, Jesus says, "If you love Me, you *will* keep My commandments" (emphasis added). This is often interpreted as a threat. However, Jesus is simply stating a fact: If we love Him, we will *want* to obey Him. The "commandments" that Jesus is referring to are not the Law, but rather the New Covenant commands of believing in Him and loving others as He loved us (1 John 3:23; John 13:34). These commands are a part of our spiritual nature, as obedience to them is imprinted on the lining of our spiritual hearts.

It's important to note that obedience is not about achieving perfect performance, but rather about growing in how we express Jesus to others. We will still make mistakes, but our hearts are programmed toward obedience. Our love for God is evident, and we naturally want to obey Him. This is the beauty of grace and obedience working together. God has transformed us from the inside out, and now our hearts are inclined toward obeying Him. We are "slaves of righteousness" and "obedient from the heart" (Romans 6:18). In short, "obedient" is a description of who we are now at the heart level. It's part of your identity in Christ: You are obedient by nature.

In conclusion, grace and obedience are not opposing concepts. Instead, they work *together* to help you grow and express Jesus even more. By God's grace, you have been given a new heart that desires to obey Him. Your love for God and others is a part of your spiritual nature. So, obedience is not about achieving perfection but about growing and learning to express who you already are!

Let's Make It a Conversation!

1. How do you understand the relationship between grace and obedience in the Christian faith? Can you give an example of a time when you felt that grace led to obedience?

2. Why do you think some people may have such a limited understanding of the power and scope of God's grace?
3. How do you respond to the idea that by God's grace, believers were given a heart that desires to obey and avoid sin? Do you agree or disagree with this statement and why?
4. Read Romans 6:14 and react to this statement: Being afraid of too much grace is like being afraid of too much obedience.

70

Is progressive sanctification a biblical concept?

Quick Answer

Progressive sanctification—the belief that believers are gradually becoming more holy over time—is *not* biblical. The Bible clearly states that believers have been sanctified (past tense) at salvation (see 1 Corinthians 6:11; 1:2; Hebrews 10:10). We're fully set apart by God and are already holy (sanctified). However, as we continue to learn and grow in our understanding of God's grace, our *behavior* is being sanctified (1 Peter 1:15). But we are not our behavior! It's crucial to understand the difference between who we are as sanctified children of God and how we conduct ourselves. The popular idea of "progressive sanctification" conflates these two. The Bible teaches us that we are made holy through the sacrifice of Jesus Christ, and this sanctification is a one-time event. While our behavior is in process, this does *not* mean we're becoming more sanctified as people. If Christ were to return in this very moment, we're fully sanctified as His children, and we're "heaven ready" with no last-minute sanctification needed.

Diving Deeper

The idea of progressive sanctification, which suggests believers are gradually becoming more sanctified with time, is not biblical. Scripture is clear that believers were sanctified in the past tense at the moment of salvation:

> Such were some of you; but you were washed, but you were sanctified, but you were justified in the name of the Lord Jesus Christ and in the Spirit of our God. (1 Corinthians 6:11)

This means we've been fully set apart by God for His purpose. Yes, our behavior is being sanctified (set apart) as we learn and grow in our understanding of God's grace (1 Peter 1:15). But it's important to separate the idea of who we are from how we perform.

Think of it this way: If Christ were to return at this moment, might we still have some learning and growing to do? Yes—and that will always be the case, because none of us will ever act perfectly. But would the Lord wait for that learning and growing to occur before taking us to Heaven? No. We are "Heaven ready" as fully sanctified (set apart) people; we belong to God in every way. When Christ returns, He will take us with Him. He will not wait for any more "setting apart" of attitudes or actions to take place first. We are sanctified people!

Unfortunately, the popular idea of progressive sanctification conflates the two types of sanctification—who we are versus what we do—and ignores what has already occurred within us as a finished work. The Bible teaches that we have been sanctified through the sacrifice of Jesus Christ, and this sanctification is a one-time event: "By this will, we have been sanctified through the offering of the body of Jesus Christ once for all time" (Hebrews 10:10). While our behavior is being sanctified, this doesn't mean we as people are becoming more holy. It simply means that our behavior is becoming more reflective of who we already are as sanctified children of God.

God is not making us more holy or sanctified as individuals. But He is working within us to help us express the reality of our newness in Christ through our attitudes and actions (Romans 12:2). As believers, we should recognize we've already been fully sanctified by God and focus on living in a way that reflects this reality.

Let's Make It a Conversation!

1. Have you come across the concept of "progressive sanctification" in your experiences? How did your understanding of the concept impact your view of growth?

2. React to this statement: A believer cannot become more sanctified (set apart) for God.

3. If we understand we're already fully sanctified, how can we apply this knowledge to our daily lives? How can we seek to live in a way that reflects this beautiful truth?

4. How might understanding our past-tense sanctification as God's people affect the way we relate to God? (Hint: Imagine not thinking of yourself as only partially ready to relate to Him!)

71
How do you become more like Christ?

Quick Answer

When we believe in Jesus, we become new creations in Him (2 Corinthians 5:17). We become like Him at the core (1 John 4:17). This means we don't need to strive to become more like Him. Instead, we can simply recognize and live out the new identity we already have in Him. Our attitudes and actions will change over time as we grow in our understanding and expression of who we are in Christ. Still, our core identity (which is like Jesus) remains the same.

Diving Deeper

A core message of Christianity is that through faith in Jesus, we are made new creations and become like Him. So we don't need to try to become more like Jesus, but rather, we can live out who we already are in Him. The Bible teaches that we're already like Jesus at the core, as we are new creations in Him (2 Corinthians 5:17) and share in His nature (1 John 4:17). This truth frees us to live out who we already are in Him, and to express Jesus in our everyday lives.

It's important to understand that Christianity is different from other religions in that we don't have to imitate a historical teacher to become more like him. Instead, the Teacher, Jesus, is alive today, living in us (Ephesians 1:13–14), and we are born of His Spirit. This means we can be ourselves and express Jesus at the same time, without any conflict.

Over time, our attitudes and actions may change as we grow in our understanding and expression of who we are in Christ, but our core identity as being like Jesus remains the same. We are God's workmanship, created for good works (Ephesians 2:10). Even though our minds are being renewed (Romans 12:2), it's crucial to recognize that we were already made new and like Jesus at salvation. With this truth in mind, we can count ourselves dead to sin and alive to God (Romans 6:11) as temptation hits. We don't have to wait to be more like Jesus in order to say *no* to sin right now. We are as dead to sin today as we will ever be!

In conclusion, while it's true that your attitudes and actions can reflect more of who you are in Christ over time, you are already like Jesus. You've been given His righteousness (2 Corinthians 5:21; Galatians 3:21; Romans 4:25; Romans 6:18). You have a new heart, a new spirit, and God's Spirit living in you. This truth frees you to live out who you already are in Him instead of trying to become something you're not yet. Christianity is unique in that the Teacher is alive today, living in us, and we can be ourselves and express Him at the exact same time, without any conflict. Remember: You're not an obstacle to God. You're His instrument!

Let's Make It a Conversation!

1. In what ways do you believe it is important to separate one's identity from his or her actions? How can this distinction impact an individual's sense of worth and righteousness?
2. How does the idea of already being like Jesus, despite not always acting like Him, resonate with you? How might this perspective shape your approach to growing in grace over time?
3. Imagine the Christian life if you were not like Jesus at the core. Wouldn't it be an invitation to fake it? Why or why not?
4. React to this statement: You're outwardly reflecting, more and more, who you already are inwardly.

72
How can you get closer to God?

Quick Answer

As believers in Jesus Christ, we're already as close to God as we can possibly be, through our union with Him and the Trinity coming to reside within us (Ephesians 1:14; Romans 6:5; John 17:23). We don't need to strive to get closer to God, as closeness is a gift of grace already given to us through Jesus's death and resurrection. Instead of trying to get closer to God, we can focus on growing in our understanding of Christ's love and His resurrection life within us. After all, we are in perfect spiritual union with Jesus Christ. This is the greatest closeness we could ever have (1 Corinthians 6:17).

Diving Deeper

As believers, we may often find ourselves wondering how we can get closer to God. We may think if we pray more, attend church more, or read the Bible more, God will draw closer to us. But this belief is not actually in agreement with the truth of the Gospel.

Here's the plain truth: when we believe in Jesus, we become one with Him, and the entire Trinity comes to live inside of us (1 Corinthians 6:17; John 14:23; John 17:23). This means we are as close to God as we can possibly be!

We are united with God in the most profound way: We are in Him, and He is in us. We are "hidden with Christ in God" (Colossians 3:3). We are one spirit with the Lord (1 Corinthians 6:17). Through Christ, we have confident access to the Father (Ephesians 2:18). The Holy Spirit also comes to live in us (John 14:17) and inspires us in our daily lives (John 16:13).

It's true that James invites his readers to "draw near to God" (James 4:8), but it's important to understand the context. James is addressing "sinners" and "double-minded" individuals who have not yet been cleansed and purified by Christ. In contrast, we believers we have been perfectly cleansed from sin (Hebrews 10:14) and are not referred to as "sinners" in Scripture. James is inviting unbelievers to "cleanse" their hands and "purify" their hearts through belief in the Gospel (James 1:21; 4:8), which will bring them to salvation and into union with Christ.

As a believer, you don't need to strive to get closer to God. You're already there. You are in perfect union with Christ and the entire Trinity (John 14:23). This closeness was not something you could achieve through your own efforts. It was a gift of grace given to you through the cross and resurrection. And it's not something you should take lightly. It's a privilege to be able to call God your Father (John 1:12). It's an honor to be able to approach Him with boldness and confidence (Hebrews 4:16), knowing you're united with His Son, Jesus Christ.

Therefore, instead of trying to get closer to God, you can focus on growing in your understanding of Him and His ways within you. You're in perfect union with the God of the Universe. That's the most intimate closeness with Him you could ever enjoy. So believe it, and be happy!

Let's Make It a Conversation!

1. How do believers sometimes try to "get closer" with God? Can you share any personal examples or experiences?
2. How do you interpret the idea that as believers, we cannot strive to get closer to God because we're already united with Christ? Can you share your thoughts on the implications of this statement?
3. How important is the distinction between growing and maturing versus attempting to "get closer" to God? Why?
4. React to this statement: God does not distance Himself when we sin. The only reason we can escape sin is because of our permanent union with Christ.

73

How can you love God more?

Quick Answer

Perhaps you've heard you need to love God more and prove your love for Him. But this concept does not appear in the New Testament. The Bible does not teach that believers need to love God more, as we already love Him to the utmost (Ephesians 6:24). The command to love God perfectly under the Law was meant to show they could not do so. Under the New Covenant, we have been given a new heart, and we've been empowered to love God and others. We love because He first loved us and poured out His love in our hearts (1 John 4:19; Romans 5:5). Our feelings (emotions) for God, church, etc., may ebb and flow, but the love in our hearts for God is an undying love (Ephesians 6:24). Rather than trying to love God more, we can grow in our understanding of His love for us (Ephesians 3:19).

Diving Deeper

Popular Christian theology often teaches that we need to love God more, but this idea is not supported by the Bible. It's true that, under the Law, people were commanded to love God perfectly with all their heart, soul, mind, and strength (Mark 12:30). But this commandment was meant to show that it was impossible for people to love God perfectly on their own and that God would have to provide a new way for us to love Him.

Under the New Covenant, loving God is not about trying to love Him more, but about believing in Jesus and loving one another (1 John 3:23; 5:4). When we believe in Jesus, we are given a new heart and a new spirit, which empowers us to love God and others (1 John 3:14; Galatians 6:10). As believers, our love for God is an undying love, because we have become obedient from the heart (Ephesians 6:24; Romans 6:17).

Instead of trying to love God more, we can rest in the reality that we already love Him with an undying love. We can wake up every day and grow in our understanding of His great love for us (Ephesians 3:19). We can also focus on living out our love for God by loving one another, as that is one of the main teachings in the New Testament (1 Corinthians 13 and 1 John 4, for example).

The beautiful reality is that God has it "rigged." Loving God is actually a perpetual state of being for the believer. Christians don't need to strive to love God more, as we already have new hearts that love Him perfectly. So our focus can be on growing in our understanding of His love for us and expressing His love to others.

Let's Make It a Conversation!

1. Have you ever felt pressure to love God more? How do you think this message differs from the truth that you *do* love God?

2. How does understanding you have an "undying love" for God change the way you approach your relationship with Him?

3. React to this statement: Trying to love God distracts us from His great love for us!

74
Does God discipline you?

Quick Answer

Many people believe that God disciplines His children because they sin, but this is inconsistent with the fact that Christ removed our sins and remembers them no more. The truth is that we are *always* under the discipline and counsel of our Father. God's discipline is training for the future, not punishment for the past. Hebrews 12 seems to liken God's discipline to scourging—the act of digging deeply into someone's back with shards of metal attached to long leather straps. Note that the Greek word (*mastigoo*) that is translated as "scourge" does mean "to scourge"—but the book of Hebrews was likely originally written in Hebrew. That would mean the Greek word *mastigoo* was a translation of the Hebrew word *biqqoret*. Interestingly, *biqqoret* can mean "to scourge" or "to deeply inquire into" (its older, original meaning). The bottom line is that God does not scourge His children, but He does deeply inquire into our lives. We are always under the loving discipline of our Father, and thank God for that!

Diving Deeper

Some think God the Father disciplines us just because we sin. But keep in mind: Jesus took away our sins, and He keeps no record of our wrongs (Hebrews 8:12; Hebrews 10:14). The reality is we're always benefitting from God's discipline, whether we've sinned recently or not.

In Hebrews 12:7–11, some interpret God's discipline as occurring because of sins committed, but the context reveals that they're being persecuted and enduring hardship. The passage states that God disciplines His children for "good, so that we may share in His holiness" (Hebrews 12:10). In other words, God disciplines us so that we continue to grow and mature in His love.

The result of this discipline is the "peaceful fruit of righteousness" (Hebrews 12:11). God's discipline leads to peace and fruit bearing. The Hebrew believers were enduring tremendous hardship (Hebrews 12:7), and the author was simply encouraging them to endure these hardships, knowing their Father was using them for good.

The most difficult portion of the passage is Hebrews 12:6, which likens God's discipline to scourging—the act of digging deeply into someone's back with shards of metal attached to long leather straps. Scourging was torture, and it was reserved only for criminals. A father never scourged his children. We see a graphic example of just how violent scourging is in Mel Gibson's film *The Passion of the Christ*, when Jesus is brutally scourged by Roman soldiers.

However, the Greek word *mastigoo* in the passage does mean "to scourge." But the book of Hebrews was likely originally written in Hebrew. That would mean that the Greek word *mastigoo* was a translation of the Hebrew word *biqqoret*. Interestingly, *biqqoret* can mean "to scourge" or "to deeply inquire into" (its original meaning). When the scourge instrument was invented much later in history, one can see why translators wanted to use the same word—scourging is "deeply inquiring into" a person's back!

The bottom line is that God does not scourge His children, but He does deeply inquire into our lives. Remember that Jesus was scourged for us, and by His stripes we are healed (Isaiah 53:5). We are always under the loving discipline of our Father. And it's through the Father's loving discipline that we experience the peaceful fruit of righteousness. God's discipline is training for the future, not punishment for the past!

Let's Make It a Conversation!

1. How do you envision God's discipline? Has your understanding been influenced by reading the perspective shared here?

2. Hebrews 8:12 says God remembers our sins no more. How does this truth shape your understanding of God's discipline and its purpose?

3. React to this statement: God's discipline is training for the future, not punishment for the past.

75

Is God breaking you or humbling you?

Quick Answer

Popular theology suggests that God is breaking or humbling us through hardships and difficult life circumstances. However, this is not biblical, as our old selves were crucified with Christ, and we have been raised with Him as new creations (Galatians 2:20; Romans 6:6; 2 Corinthians 5:17; Colossians 2:12). The Gospel teaches we're made righteous at the core of our being (Ezekiel 36:26–27; 2 Corinthians 5:21; 2 Peter 1:3–4), and our old person, the one dead in sin, has been replaced with a brand-new creation (2 Corinthians 5:17). So sin did the breaking, but God has done the transforming, and we are now complete in Christ (Colossians 2:10). He is building us up and inviting us to humble ourselves. He's not against us but for us. He is our loving Father, who wants us to be encouraged and built up in Jesus Christ through the truth of the Gospel message.

Diving Deeper

Many people believe that God breaks us or humbles us through hardships to teach us lessons. But the truth is that God is not a Dr. Death. He is Life itself, and desires for all people to experience His life abundantly (John 10:10). The idea that God is breaking or humbling us implies that there's something wrong within us that needs to be eradicated through hardship. However, this is not the truth about believers.

The Gospel teaches that when we believe in Jesus, we are spiritually crucified and buried with Christ (Galatians 2:20; Romans 6:6). We are raised with Christ in His resurrection (Colossians 2:12) and made righteous at the core of our beings (Ezekiel 36:26–27; 2 Corinthians 5:21; 2 Peter 1:3–4). Our old person, the one who was dead in sin, is obliterated and replaced with a brand-new creation (2 Corinthians 5:17). God has made us new at the core!

So it's true that our minds are still being renewed (Romans 12:1) and there are "broken" parts of our thinking and behavior that need to be transformed. But these are broken because of the fallen world's influence, not because of God. God is the healer of our minds, not the breaker. God is not seeking to "take us down a notch," but rather to encourage us.

God is inviting us to humble ourselves, just as Jesus did:

> Being found in appearance as a man, He humbled Himself by becoming obedient to death—even death on a cross! Therefore, God exalted Him to the highest place and gave Him the name that is above every name. (Philippians 2:8–9 NIV)

It's important to note that Jesus humbled Himself—and what did God do? God exalted Jesus. This shows that God was not looking to humble Jesus or teach Him a lesson through self-degradation.

God is not trying to humble us, either. The Bible confirms this through James 4:10 and 1 Peter 5:6, which say, "Humble yourselves in the presence of the Lord, and He will exalt you" and "Therefore humble yourselves under the mighty hand of God, that He may exalt you at the proper time." These verses make it clear that it's we who are doing the humbling, not God. He lovingly allows us to choose to humble ourselves—to recognize that He's God and we are dependent upon Him.

Real humility is not thinking less of ourselves. Real humility is seeing ourselves the way God sees us—no more and no less. Real humility is recognizing that we are receivers, not producers. We are dependent, not independent. Everything we have—our new self, our new heart—are not things we produced, so they're not a cause for arrogance. Everything—our forgiveness, our freedom, our new life with Jesus—was given to us by God. And the fruit of receiving these incredible gifts is humility.

In conclusion, while it may be tempting to believe that God is breaking or humbling us through difficult life circumstances, it couldn't be further from the truth. God is not breaking us; He is restoring us. He is not humbling us; He is inviting us to humble ourselves. He is not punishing us; He is disciplining us in love. He is not against us; He is for us.

God is our loving Father who desires the best for us. So let's trust in His goodness and wisdom, and rest in the truth that sets us free!

Let's Make It a Conversation!

1. In light of what we've discussed, how do you reconcile any past experiences where you felt that God was breaking

you with the understanding that He is not a breaker but an encourager?

2. Can you share an example of a difficult life circumstance that you've gone through and how your perspective on it might now be different?

3. How do the implications of the idea that God is breaking us impact our understanding of God's character and our relationship with Him? What are some potential negative effects on our well-being if we believe He is breaking us?

4. How does the concept of God humbling us align or not align with the Gospel? How does the understanding that we are truly humble now at the core of our being and that our old self is replaced with a brand-new creation change our perspective on the idea of "God humbling us"? How can this understanding bring freedom and peace?

76
How can you stay in God's will and hear His voice?

Quick Answer

God's Spirit speaks to us through the new, obedient heart and new spirit He has given us. We don't need to rely on external signs to hear from Him. Instead, we can look to Scripture and our own spiritual desires to understand His will. And the best part? We'll never fall out of God's will, because it's all about knowing and expressing Jesus in every aspect of our lives. So let go of the burdens of trying to "get" in and "stay" in God's

will, and trust that God's will is simply Jesus. Because you're
in Him, you'll never "fall out of" God's will!

Diving Deeper

It can be easy to feel like we need to rely on external means
or signs to understand God's plan for us. But the truth is
we're in union with Christ, and we can walk by faith in Him
(1 Corinthians 6:17; Galatians 2:20). Under the New Covenant,
we don't need to rely on external means to hear from God.
Instead, His Spirit communicates with us through the new,
obedient heart and new spirit He has given us (2 Peter 1:3–4;
Hebrews 8:8–12; John 4:24). This means we can experience
God inspiring us through our new spiritual desires.

In the Old Testament, God spoke audibly at times and
with visible signs. However, under the New Covenant, we can
hear from God in a new way. We don't need to guess what
God is saying; we can look to the new, righteous desires He
has implanted within us to hear from Him by faith. We can
also look to the Scriptures, which will show us clearly what
God desires for us.

You may have heard the teaching that we need to get in
God's will and then try to stay in it so we don't "fall out of"
God's will. But this can lead to a sense of burdensomeness
and ultimately, a paralysis of analysis. Thankfully, Scripture
paints a different picture of God's will. In short, the will of
God is that we know Jesus and express Him in every circumstance. And since we are always in Him, we'll never fall out
of God's will.

Scripture also offers specific insights into God's will. First, God wants all people—both Jew and Gentile—to believe and not perish (Ephesians 1:9; 3:6; 2 Peter 3:9). Second, He wills for His children to rejoice always, pray without ceasing, and give thanks in all circumstances (1 Thessalonians 5:16–18). Lastly, He desires for us to bear much fruit (John 15:8; Galatians 5:22–23).

In conclusion, we can be confident that God is working in us to fulfill His purposes, and that His agenda is to reveal our new identity in Him and His great love for us (Romans 8:16; John 16:13–14; Ephesians 3:19). Remember that God is behind every door, because Christ is always in you! And God uses all our decisions, good and bad, to form beautiful expressions of His grace over time. Simply trust in Him, and know that you're always in Jesus, so you're always "in" His will.

Let's Make It a Conversation!

1. How have you heard the idea of "finding" and "staying in" God's will taught in popular religious circles?
2. How does the New Testament actually teach us to understand God's will for our lives?
3. How does hearing from God differ today compared to the Old Testament?

PART I

THE SPIRIT AND THE CHURCH

77

Can you get more of God's Spirit through a second baptism or blessing?

Quick Answer

As a Christian, you don't need more of God's Spirit or a second baptism to experience a "second blessing." God has given every believer the full measure of the Holy Spirit at salvation. We are blessed with every spiritual blessing in Christ Jesus, and we have everything we need for life and godliness (Ephesians 1:3; 2 Peter 1:3–4). The Father, Son, and Holy Spirit indwell every believer from the moment of salvation. We are baptized into the Spirit at salvation, making us complete in Christ, and we lack nothing. This spiritual baptism is not an external event, but an internal transformation. So, you can trust in the reality of God's indwelling presence and walk in the power of His Spirit every day. Always remember that you're complete in Christ and you lack nothing.

Diving Deeper

Some argue that Christians need more of God's Spirit or a second baptism to experience a "second blessing." However, this belief is not supported by Scripture. God has given every believer the full measure of the Holy Spirit at salvation (John 14:23). We are blessed with every spiritual blessing in Christ Jesus and have everything we need for life and godliness (2 Peter 1:3–4; Ephesians 1:3).

It is important to understand that the Father, Son, and Holy Spirit indwell every believer from the moment of salvation (John 14:23; John 17:23; Ephesians 1:14). This means we already have everything we need in God. The Holy Spirit is not a force or power, but a Person who indwells us and inspires us (John 14:26). To say we need more of the Spirit is to ignore the reality of His indwelling presence within us.

Additionally, the Bible teaches that we're baptized into the Spirit at salvation (Romans 6:3–4; Colossians 2:12). This one-time event makes us complete in Christ, and we lack nothing (Colossians 2:10). We are given everything we need for life and godliness (2 Peter 1:3–4). This spiritual baptism is not an external event, but a spiritual immersion—we are hidden with Christ in God (Colossians 3:3).

Our feelings can deceive us. We may feel like we need more of God, but we must trust in the fact that He has given Himself fully and completely to us. Jesus promised that we would never hunger or thirst for more (John 6:35). This is because we've been blessed with every spiritual blessing in Christ Jesus (Ephesians 1:3) and are sealed with God's Spirit forever (Ephesians 4:30). The Holy Spirit will guide us, comfort us, empower us, and lead us in all truth.

In conclusion, you don't need more of God's Spirit or a second baptism or second blessing. You already have everything you need in the full measure of the Holy Spirit who indwells you. Yes, each one of us has a unique personality, spiritual gifts, and ways that God expresses Himself through us, but we are all equally equipped with His Spirit. He is the source of your strength, your wisdom, and your joy. He is the one who will guide you in all truth toward the life that Jesus promised. So you can trust in the reality of God's indwelling presence within you and walk in the power of the Spirit every day. You're complete in Christ and you lack nothing, because you've been blessed with every spiritual blessing in Him.

Let's Make It a Conversation!

1. How have you personally experienced the indwelling presence of the Holy Spirit in your life? (Note: This is not about a feeling but a knowing and internal leading via God's truth about who you are in Him.)

2. What are some misconceptions or false teachings you have encountered regarding the role of the Holy Spirit in the life of a believer?

3. React to this statement: Believers don't need to hunger and thirst for more of the Spirit.

4. What does it mean to you to have "every spiritual blessing" and "everything you need for life and godliness"?

78

Does the Holy Spirit convict you of sin? Can you grieve or quench Him?

Quick Answer

The Holy Spirit "convicts" unbelievers of their sins, not believers (John 16:9). The Holy Spirit convinces believers of their righteousness, and this inspires us to live upright, godly lives.

The Holy Spirit also testifies that God remembers our sins no more. Indeed, we can grieve or quench the Holy Spirit by choosing to express sin instead of the Spirit's fruit. Quenching or grieving the Spirit is not the same as God being angry with us or treating us like "convicts." Grieving or quenching the Spirit simply means God is concerned for us and wants us to fully enjoy expressing Jesus the way we're designed to.

Diving Deeper

The English word "convict" reminds many of us of a criminal who has been convicted of a crime and now sits in prison—as a convict. The Holy Spirit does not treat children of God this way. Scripture teaches that "conviction" of sin is for *unbelievers* (John 16:9). The Holy Spirit convicts unbelievers so they can find their Savior.

After we believe, the Holy Spirit does a different type of convincing within us: He convinces us of our righteousness (John 16:10) and our new identity in Christ (Romans 8:16). This is what inspires us to live godly lives. The Holy Spirit also convinces us of the reality that God remembers our sins no more (Hebrews 10:15–17).

It would be double talk to suggest the Holy Spirit simultaneously remembers our sins no more but also brings them up to "convict" us. The Holy Spirit knows and honors the finished work of Christ (Hebrews 10:15–17). He keeps no record of our wrongs but inspires us toward godly living another way: He reveals to us that we're above sin and that sin is beneath us. We're better than sin and not made for it. This is how the Spirit of God counsels us without condemnation.

But what about grieving or quenching the Spirit? To grieve the Holy Spirit is to cause Him to be deeply concerned about us (Ephesians 4:30). As a parent is concerned when their child is engaging in certain behavior patterns, so the Spirit is concerned for our well-being when He sees us living in a way that's contrary to our new identity in Him. If we choose to express sin and suppress the fruit of the Spirit, then we "quench" the Spirit (1 Thessalonians 5:19).

We're designed to bear the fruit of the Spirit and display godly qualities (2 Peter 1:3–4). So when we don't, we choose to prevent this full expression of who we are in Christ. In both the cases of quenching and grieving the Spirit, however, God is not "convicting" us like convicts. There is no guilt trip, no shame, and no condemnation. There is only gentle, loving counsel to repent (change our attitude) and express what God has designed us to express: Himself (Galatians 5:22–23).

The concept of quenching the Spirit comes on the heels of Paul describing God's will for His children. God's will is that we rejoice always, pray continually, and give thanks (1 Thessalonians 5:16–18). After this, Paul encourages the readers to not quench or prevent the Spirit from producing these within them.

The Spirit is always leading us into truth about God's nature and our own (John 16:13). It is important that we allow Him to do His beautiful work within us. The Spirit is not within us to make us feel guilty, but rather to guide us into knowing our true identity and to help us grow in Christ. When we allow the Spirit to work within us, we'll experience the fullness of joy and peace that God intends for us.

Let's Make It a Conversation!

1. How do you think understanding that the Holy Spirit remembers our sins no more can change your perspective on relationship with Him?
2. How does Revelation 12:10 influence your understanding of how the Holy Spirit treats us in comparison to Satan?
3. In your own words, what does it mean to quench or grieve the Holy Spirit? How is this different from the Spirit being angry or giving you a guilt trip?

79

What does it mean to "walk by the Spirit"?

Quick Answer

Walking by the Spirit means relying on the Holy Spirit to produce His fruit in our lives. All Christians are already in the Spirit as a result of our salvation and union with Christ. However, we're called to make choices that align with the Holy Spirit and enjoy a life that expresses Him. Walking by the Spirit is about living daily from our union with Christ and making decisions that are in line with His counsel. As Galatians 5:25 says "If we live by the Spirit, let us also walk by the Spirit."

Diving Deeper

Galatians 5:16 instructs us to "walk by the Spirit." This means we are to trust in the work of Christ in us and allow the Holy Spirit to produce the fruit of the Spirit within us. The fruit of the Spirit, as listed in Galatians 5:22–23, includes love, joy, peace, patience, kindness, goodness, faithfulness, gentleness, and self-control.

It's important to note that we are always *in* the Spirit. This is a result of our salvation and our union with Christ. As Romans 8:9 states, "You are not in the flesh but *in* the Spirit, if indeed the Spirit of God dwells in you" (emphasis added). And in John 17:23, Jesus prays that we would be one with Him as He is one with the Father. We are forever bonded to the Holy Spirit, and we cannot receive more of the Spirit over time. Ephesians 1:14 states that we are marked in Him with a seal, the promised Holy Spirit.

Because we are always in the Spirit, we are called to make choices that are compatible with Him to enjoy a life that expresses Him. As 1 Corinthians 6:17 states, "But the one who joins himself to the Lord is one spirit with Him." And Titus 3:5 reminds us that we've been saved by the washing of regeneration and renewal by the Holy Spirit. So it only makes sense to express the Spirit.

In summary, walking by the Spirit is about living daily from your union with Christ and making decisions in step with Him. It's not about becoming more "in" the Spirit or receiving more of the Spirit over time. It's about allowing the Spirit that already lives within you to produce His fruit through your unique personality. As Galatians 5:25 says, "If we live by the Spirit, let us also *walk* by the Spirit" (emphasis added).

Let's Make It a Conversation!

1. In your own words, can you explain what it means to walk "by" the Spirit in contrast to simply being "in" the Spirit?
2. How do you reconcile the idea of still being "in" the Spirit while also committing a sin? Can you share an example from your own life that illustrates this concept?
3. React to this statement: Walking by the Spirit is natural for someone who is born of the Spirit. Doing anything else goes against the very fiber of their being.

80

What does it mean to be "filled with the Spirit"?

Quick Answer

Being "filled with the Spirit" is not about receiving a special spiritual gift or an extra anointing. It's about letting the immense love of Christ inspire and guide our actions. Ephesians 5:18–21 states that we are to be continuously filled with the Spirit, and Ephesians 3:18–19 explains that this means knowing the love of Jesus. The powerful love of Christ brings us peace, relaxation, and inspiration. The book of Acts illustrates how those "filled with the Spirit" (inspired by the love of Christ) shared the Gospel, served others, and stood up for the truth. The love of Jesus is the foundation of our faith and the driving force behind our actions. Christ's love is what inspires us to live a life of purpose and joy!

Diving Deeper

Many people believe being "filled with the Spirit" is about having certain spiritual gifts such as tongues or prophecy, and that it's a second blessing or an extra anointing. However, the Bible is clear that being "filled with the Spirit" is about knowing the love of Christ and being inspired by His great love.

Ephesians 5:18–21 is the only New Testament passage that explicitly commands Christians to be "filled with the Spirit." The Greek literally means "be being filled." In other words, Paul is saying we already have the Spirit, but now we can allow the Spirit to continuously inspire us. But how do we let the Spirit influence us? The answer is found in Ephesians 3:18–19, where Paul says believers can know the love of Christ and thereby be filled with all the "fullness of God." So being "filled with the Spirit" means knowing the love of Christ.

Paul compares being filled with the Spirit to being drunk on wine. Just as people look to too much wine to relax them and give them peace, the love of Christ does the same for us. To be "filled with the Spirit" is to find relaxation, peace, and inspiration from the enormous love of God.

The book of Acts cites examples of people who were "filled with the Spirit" (inspired by God's love) and then shared the Gospel in human languages (Acts 2:4), addressed rulers with boldness (Acts 4:8), spoke the Word of God with confidence (Acts 4:31), served food at tables (Acts 6:3), preached to those who persecuted them (Acts 7:55), encouraged people with the Gospel (Acts 11:24), challenged deceivers (Acts 13:52), and experienced joy despite persecution (Acts 13:52). Notice the variety of actions taken when "filled with the Spirit" (inspired by the love of Christ).

In conclusion, being "filled with the Spirit" does not mean getting more of God's presence through a second portion or second blessing. It's not about a particular spiritual gift. It's about knowing and trusting Christ's love, and that is the birthright and destiny of every child of God. The love of Christ is what compels us to bear fruit, serve others, and live a life of purpose and joy in Him.

Let's Make It a Conversation!

1. How had you previously understood the concept of "being filled with the Spirit" based on popular teachings and experiences?

2. How does the passage in Ephesians 3:18–19 provide insight into the meaning of "being filled with the Spirit" as mentioned in Ephesians 5?

3. React to this statement: Being filled with the Spirit is not about getting more of the Spirit. It's about the ongoing adventure of being inspired by Christ's love.

81

What does "praying in the Spirit" mean? Does God only hear certain prayers?

Quick Answer

Praying in the Spirit is simply praying with the confidence that we are "in" the Spirit and He is in us. We're acknowledging that we're in union with Christ and one with God. It means recognizing our location in Christ and that we already have a perfect connection with Him. Our human spirits are already in conversation with the Holy Spirit all day long. He hears us every time we pray, regardless of our recent performance. So let's pray with confidence, knowing that we are righteous, and our prayers are *always* heard by our loving Father. Embrace and cherish the privilege of praying, because you're *in* God's Spirit.

Diving Deeper

Ephesians 6:18 tells us to pray in the Spirit, but what does that really mean? Some may interpret it as speaking in tongues or praying in a special way to God. But the truth is, the phrase is simply talking about our location with God. We are always "in" the Spirit, and therefore we can consciously pray with our closeness to God in mind.

When we pray, we can acknowledge that we're in union with Christ and that we're one with God. John 17:23 tells us that Christians are "in" God, and this is our new location from the moment we believe. We are never "out" of God.

This is why we're told that we're "hidden with Christ in God" (Colossians 3:3) and that we're seated with Christ in heavenly places (Ephesians 2:6). We're as close to Jesus as we can get!

Praying in the Spirit is not about speaking in tongues or praying in a special way, but about recognizing our location in Christ and that we're already one with God. Romans 8:16 tells us that our human spirits are already in conversation with the Holy Spirit, and He knows what we're asking before we even ask it. He even prays on our behalf (Romans 8:26). So praying in the Spirit is not about trying to speak in a language that only God can understand. It's about recognizing that we're already in perfect communication with Him.

Now, some may think James 5:16 (which states that the prayers of righteous people are powerful and effective) means God only hears certain prayers. Absolutely not! James is saying that the prayers of a believer, who is the righteousness of God (2 Corinthians 5:21), are highly effective. This passage is meant to be an encouragement to believers, not to invoke anxious introspection as to whether we are righteous enough for God to hear us. We are already perfect tens because of the finished work of Jesus Christ. We are the righteousness of God, and we are His children. He hears us every time we pray, regardless of our recent performance.

In conclusion, praying in the Spirit is not about speaking in tongues or praying in a special way, but about recognizing your location in Christ and that you're already one with God. So, you can pray with confidence, knowing you're already in perfect communication with the Holy Spirit and that He always hears your prayers. Praying in the Spirit is a powerful reality that we can embrace and cherish.

Let's Make It a Conversation!

1. In your own words, what is praying in the Spirit? Did this discussion change your view of praying in the Spirit?

2. Does knowing you're righteous and that your prayers are *always* heard by God help you pray with confidence? Share your thoughts.

3. In what ways can you recognize and acknowledge your location in Christ when you pray, and how might this enhance your understanding and experience of prayer?

82
What is the gift of prophecy?

Quick Answer

The gift of prophecy is one of the most misunderstood topics in Christianity. Many believe New Testament prophecy is future-telling or speaking the secret truths of God. However, the New Testament defines the gift of prophecy as God equipping someone to share the truths of the Gospel for the purpose of edification, exhortation, and consolation (1 Corinthians 14:3).

Diving Deeper

While there's a lot of debate surrounding prophecy, 1 Corinthians 14:3 clearly defines the gift of prophecy for us.

It says the gift is meant for "edification and exhortation and consolation."

Edification means to build someone up by speaking truth to them. Exhortation is spurring others on to new thinking and new actions. Consolation is comforting someone in a time of need. What particular words edify, exhort, and console a person? The message of the Gospel itself, of course.

So, prophecy is not someone laying hands on you and predicting your future. Nor is it someone communicating "secret truths" from God about your life that you'd otherwise miss. Instead, prophecy is a loving brother or sister in Christ applying the amazing truths of the Gospel message to you, in your situation, and for your benefit. Consider a Christian counselor, for example, who is aware of someone's struggle and is equipped by God to offer insights from the truth of the Gospel that directly apply to that person's life. They may have the gift of prophecy that enables them to first console, then edify, then exhort in a way that brings healing (1 Corinthians 14:3).

Furthermore, the gift of prophecy does not involve someone mindlessly speaking the thoughts of God while out of control. No, Paul told the Corinthians the opposite—that "the spirits of prophets are subject to the control of prophets" (1 Corinthians 14:32 NIV). The gift of prophecy is never an out-of-control experience, and all spiritual gifts are to be used in an orderly manner for the benefit of others.

In summary, the gift of prophecy involves a practical application of the truth of the Gospel to someone's life. It's not about predicting the future or communicating secret truths, but rather speaking the truth of the Gospel in a way that builds up, encourages, and comforts others.

In conclusion, the gift of prophecy is a powerful tool for the Church, and when used in a healthy manner, it can bring about tremendous growth and maturity in the Body of Christ. It is beautiful when someone uses the gift of prophecy in a way that edifies, exhorts, and consoles others, bringing glory to God and building up His Kingdom.

Let's Make It a Conversation!

1. How has your understanding of the gift of prophecy developed over time? Have you had any personal experiences or encounters that have shaped your perspective on this topic?

2. In what ways do you see the role of prophecy in the New Testament as distinct from the predictions made by Old Testament prophets? How does 1 Corinthians 14:3 help to clarify this difference?

3. How does the warning in Revelation 22:19 impact your understanding of the authority and authenticity of prophetic utterances in the church today?

4. How do you see the role of prophecy in the New Testament as similar or different from the role of a Christian counselor? What are the benefits or limitations of this analogy? Are there any other ways in which you would describe the function of prophecy in the church?

83

What is the gift of tongues?

Quick Answer

The gift of tongues is a hotly debated topic, with many believing it's a way to communicate with God in an angelic language. But the true purpose of tongues, as seen in the Bible, is to share the Gospel message with nonbelievers in their own language. In Acts 2, we see the apostles using this gift to reach a multitude of people and lead them to salvation. This is the only instance in Scripture where we are shown the "content" of tongue speaking. To conclude that speaking in tongues involves a heavenly or angelic language is to introduce a concept that is simply not found anywhere in Acts or in the epistles. Tongues was (and still is) used to persuade unbelievers that God is powerful and miraculous and to allow them to hear the Gospel message—that He sent Jesus Christ to offer them salvation.

Diving Deeper

The gift of tongues is often misunderstood as speaking in an angelic or heavenly language for the purpose of communicating with God and building up oneself. However, the true biblical gift of tongues is sharing the Gospel message with unbelievers in their own language.

In Acts 2, we see the apostles speaking in tongues to a multitude of people who hear the Gospel message in their own native languages. Many of these people consequently believed the message and were saved. This is the only instance in Scripture where we are shown the "content" of tongue speaking. To conclude that speaking in tongues involves babbling in a heavenly language is to introduce a concept that is simply not found in the New Testament.

Paul's 1 Corinthians 13 reference to speaking with the tongues "of angels" is hyperbole for the purpose of showcasing the importance of love and is unrelated to the gift of tongues. This is why Paul also mentioned moving mountains and giving his body to be burned. He was simply saying that love is more important than any of these. He was in no way claiming that he actually moved mountains, gave his body to be burned, or spoke an angelic language.

Lastly, Paul's reference in Jude 1:20 to "praying in the Holy Spirit" relates to praying with the confidence that we have bold access (in the Spirit) to God Himself. This was a newsflash for New Testament believers, as this vine-branches relationship with God's Spirit had never been experienced before. It's important to note that Jude 1 says we should *always* pray in this way. Therefore, praying in the Spirit is *not* a second way to pray. It's the only way to pray! And the context of the Jude 1 passage has nothing to do with the gift of tongues.

Much has been made of 1 Corinthians 14:2, which talks about speaking mysteries that only God understands. Many have argued that Paul is advocating for speaking these mysteries to God. However, the context of 1 Corinthians 14 is corporate worship, and Paul is actually forbidding the Corinthians from speaking in a tongue when only God understands. He urges them to speak with both the spirit and their mind and to speak in a way that benefits other people in church. This is why, later in the chapter, he states that if an interpreter is not present, the speaker should be silent and not interrupt the church service (1 Corinthians 14:28). This further emphasizes that the purpose of speaking in tongues is for the edification of others, not for private prayer.

In summary, the gift of tongues is a missionary gift for the purpose of evangelism in foreign languages, just as we see in Acts 2. This is why the gift of tongues is called a sign for the unbeliever, not for the believer (see 1 Corinthians 14:22). Those who claim that a second type of tongues exists as a private prayer language say it is to edify themselves. But we are explicitly told that spiritual gifts are for the edification of others, not ourselves (Ephesians 4:12). Additionally, many who support the idea of a private prayer language are eager to teach this language to others through repetition or helping them along. However, spiritual gifts are never the result of imitation or instruction. Spiritual gifts are distributed by the Holy Spirit to the church at His discretion (1 Corinthians 12:7; Romans 12:3–8), and there is a beautiful variety and diversity of gifts in the Body of Christ (1 Corinthians 12:28–30).

Let's Make It a Conversation!

1. How has your previous understanding of the gift of tongues evolved or changed?
2. In what ways does the account of the gift of tongues in Acts 2:8 provide insight into its purpose and function?

3. What could be some reasons for the gift of tongues being both highly valued and highly divisive?

4. React to this statement: It's more important to speak in love than to speak in tongues.

84
Should the Lord's Supper be a "closed" ceremony?

Quick Answer

The Lord's Supper is a time for us to reflect on the finished work of Christ and to remember His sacrifice for our sins. However, some churches practice a "closed communion" in which only certain people are allowed to participate. But the idea of a "closed communion" is not scriptural, and we should want children, visitors, and everyone to participate in the celebration of Jesus's finished work.

Diving Deeper

The Lord's Supper, or Communion, is an important practice that commemorates the death of Jesus Christ on the cross. It is a time for us to reflect on the finished work of Christ and to remember His sacrifice for our sins. However, some denominations or groups practice a "closed communion," restricting children, visitors, etc., from participating.

The Bible does not contain any passage that says we should prevent people from celebrating the body and blood of Jesus. In fact, the Bible encourages us to share the truth about Jesus with others. In 1 Corinthians 11:24, Paul writes, "and when He had given thanks, He broke it and said, 'This is *My body, which is for you*; do this in remembrance of Me'" (emphasis added). This passage shows that the Lord's Supper is for everyone Jesus gave His life for, not just a select few.

Some churches teach we need to make sure there are no unconfessed sins in our life before we take communion. However, this is not what the "examination" in 1 Corinthians 11 is really about. The passage is about how the church in Corinth was getting drunk on wine and eating too much food during the Lord's Supper while others (the poor) went hungry (1 Corinthians 11:29–30; 1 Corinthians 11:21). For this reason, there were divisions among them (1 Corinthians 11:18). They needed to examine their practices at the Lord's Supper, *not* their recent track record over the last week or month! So, it was never about excluding people from communion because of their sinful performance disqualifying them. Remember that James says we all struggle in many ways (James 3:2). To be consistent, if we exclude one person because of a struggle with sin, then we'd have to exclude everyone.

Another issue is excluding children from taking communion. This practice is unwarranted. Children are precious to Jesus, and He wants them to think of Him at every opportunity (Matthew 19:14). Who knows if a child might hear the Gospel message, believe it, and be saved during the celebration of the Lord's Supper? Why would we want to prevent that? We also see churches exclude people because they do not belong to their denomination or religious organization. However, the concept of church membership is not supported biblically. We are a kingdom of priests and members of God's global Church because we believe in Jesus.

In conclusion, the idea of a "closed communion" is not biblical. God wants all people to reflect on the finished work of Christ. And if we exclude someone, then we may very well be interfering with their salvation. We should want children, visitors, and everyone to focus on the finished work of Christ and to participate in a Lord's Supper celebration.

Let's Make It a Conversation!

1. How do you feel about the idea of excluding certain individuals from participating in the Lord's Supper, and why do you feel that way? Have you ever personally struggled with this concept or encountered it in your church community?

2. In what ways do you think participating in the Lord's Supper can benefit those who do not yet believe in Jesus (visitors, children, etc.)?

3. What are some possible reasons or motivations behind the practice of closed communion within certain denominations or churches? How might this concept be challenged or reevaluated in light of the wide-open Gospel invitation?

85

Is it necessary to go to church?

Quick Answer

Hebrews encourages Christians to gather together as believers for the purpose of uplifting and encouraging each other in the truth of the Gospel. This doesn't mean that formal church services are the only way to do this, but rather that we should thrive in community with other trusted Christian friends. John's experience of living alone on the Isle of Patmos is not the normal Christian life. We are meant to be in fellowship with one another. Community can happen in various ways, such as a coffee shop gathering, a dinner and discussion event, or an online Bible study group. The important thing is that we find people to walk with through life. Gathering together as the Body of Christ is not about fulfilling a religious duty, but about fulfilling our purpose as members of the Body of Christ.

Diving Deeper

Hebrews 10:25 urges us not to forget the power of gathering together as believers. This doesn't mean we have to attend a formal church service on Sunday mornings, but rather that we are meant to thrive in community with other trusted Christian friends. We come together to uplift and encourage each other in the truth of the Gospel.

John's experience of living in isolation on the Isle of Patmos, where he received the visions recorded in the book of Revelation, is not the norm or even the ideal for a Christian life. We are meant to be in fellowship with one another. It's important to remember that John's time on the Isle of Patmos was temporary, and he had opportunities to connect with other believers throughout his life. We are not meant to be "Lone Ranger" Christians.

The author of Hebrews encourages us to not neglect meeting together (Hebrews 10:25). God isn't making a rule saying we have to attend church to be more righteous or closer to Him (1 Corinthians 6:17). Instead, He's simply speaking to our innate need for community with others who know Jesus, too.

Community can happen in various ways, such as a coffee shop gathering, a dinner and discussion event, or an online Bible study group. The important thing is that we find people to walk with through life. Healthy community provides us with the support we need during life's highs and lows, and allows us to love others with the love we've received from Christ (John 13:34).

The idea of "going to church" is often seen as a legalistic burden or obligation. This is not what God intended for His people when He called us to gather with other believers. Legalism is the erroneous belief that we can earn or maintain our status with God through our own actions, rather than by grace through faith in Jesus Christ (Ephesians 2:8–9). The Bible speaks of the Church as a family—and as members of this family, we have the opportunity to love and support one another as we journey through life together (Ephesians 2:19). In this sense, gathering together is not about fulfilling a religious duty, but about fulfilling our purpose as members of the Body of Christ and the family of God.

In conclusion, Christians don't have to "go to church" out of guilt or duty but can gather with other believers with a heartfelt desire to encourage each other. The Bible encourages us not to neglect meeting together, because it's an opportunity to grow and be built up by others. Gathering as the church is not about earning points with God, but about fulfilling our purpose as members of His family.

Let's Make It a Conversation!

1. According to Hebrews 10:25, what is the main purpose of gathering together as a community of believers?
2. How does the Bible's message about the purpose of gathering with other believers differ from the societal notion of "attending church" as a legalistic burden or obligation? How can this understanding prevent the abuse of quantifying and measuring one's spiritual status through church attendance?
3. React to this statement: We are the church, so church can be anywhere at any time.

MARRIAGE, SEX, AND GENDER

86

Can Christians get divorced?

Quick Answer

Divorce can be a painful experience, but it's important to remember that God recognizes there are certain circumstances in which it is necessary. The Bible has a lot to say about this topic, and it's essential to understand what it says. For example, in Exodus 21:10–11, it states that if a wife is deprived of her basic needs and rights, she may "go out for nothing, without payment of money." This passage is describing an abusive situation, and God still wants to protect us from abuse today. Additionally, the word for "divorce" in 1 Corinthians 7 actually refers to abandoning a spouse without a certificate of divorce, which would not enable them to remarry. Here, Paul is not disallowing divorce for Christians, but rather instructing them to only divorce in a legal manner so that their spouse is respected in society and free to remarry.

Diving Deeper

Divorce can be a difficult and painful experience for anyone, especially for those who are believers. It can be easy to feel like an outcast in God's family if you've been through a divorce. But the truth is that there are times when divorce is needed, and God has not abandoned us.

God does intend marriage to last a lifetime. In Matthew 19:6, Jesus says, "What God has joined together, let no one separate" (NIV). This passage reflects Christ's faithfulness to the Church and the way God loves us unconditionally. But even in the Old Testament, God recognized there are certain circumstances in which divorce is necessary.

For example, Exodus 21:10–11 states that if a wife is deprived of "her food, her clothing, or her conjugal rights," she may go "out for nothing without payment of money." This passage is describing a genuinely abusive situation, in which the husband is neglecting his wife's basic needs and rights. Today, we may still apply this concept to modern-day marriage. If a spouse is being abused in some way or having their "marital rights" threatened, then divorce may be the healthiest option. God doesn't want His children to remain in harmful or abusive relationships. Think about it: If God was merciful to Israel under the Law, is He any less merciful to us under grace today?

Jesus's teachings in Matthew 19 are often misinterpreted as completely outlawing divorce for Christians. However, in this passage, Jesus is actually addressing a question from the Jews about His stance on divorce in relation to two schools of thought: Hillel and Shamai. Jesus aligns Himself with the stricter interpretation of the school of Shamai, stating that divorce is only permissible in cases of infidelity. In this way, Jesus does not give His Jewish hearers an "out" with their loose interpretation of the Law and their poor treatment of women; the Pharisees were notoriously misogynistic, and this attitude was reflected in many of the hundreds of rules they added to the Jewish tradition. Instead, Jesus leans in and doubles down on what the Law says, and thus convicts them of their cruel behavior toward women. This passage should be seen much like the Sermon on the Mount. It's not binding on Christians (who are not under the Law) but instead demonstrated the hypocrisy of the Pharisees who touted their Law-keeping yet broke the Law anytime it suited them.

Another circumstance in which divorce may be necessary is when an unbeliever leaves the marriage. In 1 Corinthians 7, Paul encourages the believing spouse to let the person leave without a fight. Furthermore, it's also important to note that the word for "divorce" used in 1 Corinthians 7:11 actually means to "send away" a spouse *without* a certificate of divorce that would enable them to remarry. This is supported by the grammar in the passage, as only the husband could issue the certificate, and the language used for the wife is passive, implying that she is a recipient of the action rather than the initiator. Here, Paul is not prohibiting divorce for Christians, but rather encouraging them to divorce legally in order to free women to remarry. This was more respectful than just sending them away.

In conclusion, God intends marriage to last a lifetime in order to reflect His unconditional love for us. However, He also recognizes that there are circumstances in which divorce is necessary, such as neglect and abuse. If you find yourself in a difficult marriage, know that you are not alone and that God is with you. And if you decide to divorce, remember that you are still a beloved child of God, and He has not abandoned or disqualified you from contributing to the Body of Christ. You are the righteousness of God because of Jesus's death and resurrection, not because of your marital status!

Let's Make It a Conversation!

1. How has the church community you are familiar with handled and addressed the topic of divorce? What has been your personal experience with this within the church?

2. How might understanding the concept of "putting away a spouse without a certificate" in 1 Corinthians 7 change one's perspective on divorce?

3. In what ways might understanding this viewpoint change the way you offer guidance and support to individuals facing a potential divorce or those who are already divorced?

87

Can a divorced Christian get remarried?

Quick Answer

Divorce can be a difficult and emotional experience for Christians, and some may believe God forbids remarriage after a divorce. However, this is not an accurate view of Scripture. The Bible teaches that believers are completely forgiven for all sins, including adultery, through the finished work of the cross. This means that if you've been divorced, any sins committed—including adultery—have been completely taken away by the finished work of the cross. This frees you to marry again and form a healthy, Christ-centered relationship with your new spouse. You are fully forgiven, completely loved, and never forsaken. So, if you have been divorced, you can lean into the love and grace of God as you navigate this difficult time in your life.

Diving Deeper

Some Christians believe God forbids remarriage after a divorce, but this is not an accurate view of the whole of Scripture. God's grace is big enough to handle any failed marriage and to empower us to have a new and healthy marriage going forward.

The Bible teaches that believers are completely forgiven for all sins, including adultery, through the finished work of the cross (Hebrews 8:12; 14; Ephesians 4:32; Colossians 3:13). Therefore, if we've been divorced, any sins committed, including adultery (1 Corinthians 6:9–11), have been completely taken away through the finished work of the cross. We are free to marry again and form a healthy new relationship with a believing person.

Some might cite Matthew 5:32 and Matthew 19:9, in which Jesus teaches that marrying a divorced person is adultery. However, in both of these cases, He was addressing the Jews under the Law. First, in Matthew 5, we find Jesus saying this alongside His other instruction to cut off your hand, pluck out your eye, and be perfect like God. It's clear this entire passage (Matthew 5:17–48) is designed to show what perfect Law-keeping really looked like and how far from the standard the Jews really were.

Likewise, in Matthew 19, the Pharisees come to Jesus to test Him. But Jesus turns the tables on them by showcasing their hypocrisy and inability to treat women respectfully. (The Pharisees would often "put away" their wives without a certificate of divorce and then marry someone new whenever they wanted.) In both cases—Matthew 5 and Matthew 19—Jesus is addressing those under the Law to show them what was really required. However, we believers today are *not* under the Law. Jesus fulfilled the Law so that we wouldn't have to!

In summary, while the Bible acknowledges that divorce can happen due to sin and brokenness, it does not prohibit remarriage. Instead, it encourages believers to seek forgiveness, healing, and restoration, and allows for the possibility of remarriage. Ultimately, God's grace and forgiveness through the finished work of the cross extends to all believers, regardless of their marital status, and empowers them to move forward in healthy relationships.

It's important for Christians who have gone through a divorce and are considering remarriage to seek healing and restoration for any past issues, and to ensure that their new relationship is healthy and centered on Christ. And it's important to remember that God's grace and forgiveness can empower us to move forward in a confident and fulfilling way.

Let's Make It a Conversation!

1. How has your understanding of the possibility of remarriage after divorce changed or been affected by beliefs within your community?
2. How can we as the Church better support and uplift those who have gone through divorce and may be considering remarriage in the future?

3. How does the true Gospel message inspire us to extend grace to those who have gone through divorce and are navigating the possibility of remarriage?

88

Is it alright to have sex before marriage?

Quick Answer

The Bible teaches that sex and marriage were created to be one and the same by God's design. In Genesis 2:24 and Mark 10:8–10, sexual union is associated with becoming one with your spouse, emphasizing the importance of marriage commitment. Society may view sex as something that can happen outside of marriage, but this goes against God's plan. True fulfillment in sex can only be found within the sanctity of marriage. As a believer, you're totally forgiven, but it's possible to be forgiven yet miserable inside! That's why God wants you to find true joy in Him and His plan for sex and marriage.

Diving Deeper

The Bible teaches that sex and marriage are intimately connected, and that God's design for sex is within the context of marriage. Genesis 2:24 states,

> For this reason a man shall leave his father and his mother, and be joined to his wife; and they shall become one flesh.

This passage not only emphasizes the importance of leaving one's family to start a new one, but also the concept of "becoming one flesh" which is a reference to sexual union. This verse makes it clear that sexual union is an important part of the marriage commitment.

Mark 10:8–10 also highlights the connection between sex and marriage:

> And the two shall become one flesh; so they are no longer two, but one flesh. What therefore God has joined together, let no man separate.

This passage emphasizes that God has joined the two together, and that sex is an integral part of that union.

In contrast, modern society perpetuates many lies about marriage, one of which is the idea that sex can exist independently of marriage. People are encouraged to engage in premarital sex and to view it as a casual and insignificant act. However, this is not in line with God's design. When sex is dissociated from marriage, it loses its purpose of helping someone become one with another person and forming a committed union. The concept of "sex before marriage" is an oxymoron, as it goes against God's original vision for sex.

Furthermore, engaging in premarital sex can lead to a host of problems. It can cause emotional turmoil, lead to broken relationships, and even have physical consequences like disease. God wants us to avoid this pain. His plan for sex is beautiful and fulfilling, but it's only meant to be experienced within the context of marriage.

It's also important to remember that as a believer, you're a totally forgiven person (Hebrews 10:14), and God looks at you as if you've never sinned a day in your life. However, even though you're forgiven, God doesn't want you to be forgiven yet *miserable*. That's why, going forward, His Spirit will guide you away from the confusion of premarital sex. God wants you to find true fulfillment in Him.

In conclusion, sex and marriage are intimately connected, and God's design for sex is within the context of marriage. The Bible teaches that sexual union is an important part of the marriage commitment, and that sex is meant to be experienced within the context of marriage. Modern society's perpetuation of the idea that sex can exist independently of marriage is not in line with God's plan. He wants us to find true fulfillment in Him and to see the wisdom in His ways.

Let's Make It a Conversation!

1. How does God's design for sex and marriage differ from the societal view of sex as something that can happen outside of marriage? What are the purposes of sex within the context of marriage?
2. In what ways can engaging in premarital sex lead to turmoil (emotional, psychological, etc.)?
3. How does the gospel of grace and our new identity in Christ speak into sex and marriage today?

89

Is masturbation always wrong?

Quick Answer

Masturbation is not mentioned in Scripture and is considered a matter of conscience. While some may interpret a passage in Genesis 38 as relating to masturbation, it's actually about a man's failure to fulfill his duty as a kinsman redeemer. It's important to remember that Scripture states that sexual lust is a sin, so if masturbation is combined with pornography or fantasy, it is sinful. However, many well-respected Christian theologians and therapists believe it's possible to masturbate without sinning. It's important to have open and honest conversations with your spouse about masturbation, as it should not harm a marriage. Ultimately, it's up to each individual to make a wise decision about masturbation through the counsel of God's Spirit.

Diving Deeper

While pornography and sexual fantasy are clearly sinful, the physical act of masturbation is not mentioned in Scripture and seems to be a matter of conscience for each believer. However, there are a few biblical references that can provide guidance on the matter.

In Genesis 38:9, Onan spills his seed instead of impregnating his deceased brother's widow to carry on the family line. Some point to this passage and relate it to masturbation.

However, this is an interpretive leap as the passage is not about masturbation at all, but rather about Onan's failure to fulfill his duty as a kinsman redeemer (Genesis 38:8–10).

While Scripture does not directly address masturbation, there are a few obvious truths we can use to ensure that the act is not sinful for us. First, the New Testament is clear that sexual lust is a sin. It stands to reason that when lust is combined with masturbation, such as when pornography or fantasy are included, then masturbation is sinful. However, many Christian theologians, counselors, and therapists believe it's possible to masturbate solely as a physical release without sinning (though for many, it's nearly impossible due to the sinful habits they've formed with pornography or fantasy).

In a marriage, it's crucial that the spouse be involved in the conversation about masturbation. Husbands and wives are sexual partners (1 Corinthians 7:5) and are to be intimately involved in each other's sexuality. If masturbating hurts our spouse or our marriage in any way, then we need to steer clear of it. God wants us to enjoy a healthy marriage filled with desire for our spouse.

Masturbation might be perfectly healthy for some—such as a single person, spouses who spend much time apart, or those who are in a difficult family situation where a spouse is sick. However, it can easily turn into something sinful for anyone who has a history of associating the act of masturbation with pornography, fantasy, and lust.

Let's Make It a Conversation!

1. Some view masturbation as a sin, while others may dis-agree, especially when pornography, fantasy, and lust are absent. How do you personally view masturbation?

2. How have your experiences with masturbation, if any, affected your overall well-being? Is there any context in which you see yourself giving thanks to God for it? Why or why not?

3. How do you think masturbation should be addressed within the dynamics of singleness and marriage?

90

Is being gay considered a sin?

Quick Answer

God intended for men and women to have sexual intimacy with each other in a marital relationship (Genesis 1–2). But after sin entered the world (Genesis 3), this original design was distorted and led to homosexual practices, which are condemned in the Old Testament (Leviticus 18:22; 20:13) and in the New Testament (Romans 1:26–27). In Romans 1, homosexuality is portrayed as a result of rejecting God's plan for sexuality and is described as unnatural and a source of shame. Contrary to some interpretations, these passages do not only refer to abusive or distorted forms of homosexuality, but instead describe any form of same-sex relations. Romans 1:26–27 states that men and women abandoned natural sexual relationships and became inflamed with lust for each other. While homosexuality may be a current hot-topic issue, it is just one form of sin among many. Romans 1 reminds us that all humans are equally condemned and have no right to judge others. The only way to find true identity is by belonging to Jesus Christ.

Diving Deeper

God designed men and women to have intimate sexual relations within the boundaries of marriage (Genesis 1–2). This design was meant to reflect the love and unity between Christ and the Church. However, after sin entered the world (Genesis 3), God's original design was distorted and led to practices that are condemned in Scripture. One such practice is homosexuality.

Homosexuality is considered to be sin in both the Old Testament (Leviticus 18:22; 20:13) and the New Testament (Romans 1:26–27). Romans 1 is particularly significant as it gives insight into why homosexuality is seen as sinful. In this chapter, Paul describes how humanity turned away from God and began to engage in unnatural sexual practices. The abandonment of natural sexual relationships for unnatural ones is described as exchanging the truth about God for a lie (Romans 1:25). Men and women gave themselves over to shameful lusts and committed shameful acts with each other (Romans 1:26–27).

Despite efforts by some to argue that these passages only refer to distorted forms of homosexuality, such as rape, this interpretation does not hold up in the context of Romans 1.

In this chapter, Paul is not referring to rape but is instead describing the rejection of God's plan for sexuality. This rejection is described as exchanging natural sexual relationships for unnatural ones, such as men having sexual relations with other men and women with other women.

Paul makes it clear that homosexuality is not in line with God's plan for sexuality when he writes in 1 Corinthians 6:9–10,

> Or do you not know that the unrighteous will not inherit the kingdom of God? Do not be deceived; neither fornicators, nor idolaters, nor adulterers, nor effeminate, nor homosexuals, nor thieves, nor the covetous, nor drunkards, nor revilers, nor swindlers, will inherit the kingdom of God.

In 1 Timothy 1:9–10, Paul goes on to say,

> Realizing the fact that law is not made for a righteous person, but for those who are lawless and rebellious, for the ungodly and sinners, for the unholy and profane, for those who kill their fathers or mothers, for murderers and immoral men and homosexuals and kidnappers and liars and perjurers, and whatever else is contrary to sound teaching.

It is clear from these passages that homosexuality is seen as sinful in both the Old and New Testaments. However, it is important to note that while homosexuality is one form of sin, it is by no means the only form. There are many other ways in which humanity has rejected God's plan and turned to sin. This is why in Romans 1:30 homosexuality is listed alongside "disobedience to parents."

The overarching message of Romans 1 is that all humans are equally condemned and have no right to judge others. We're all sinners in need of the grace and forgiveness that can only be found in Jesus Christ. It is through faith in Him that we can find true fulfillment and purpose.

In conclusion, while homosexuality is seen as sinful in Scripture, it's just one of the many ways in which humanity has rejected God's plan. The solution to all forms of sin is the same: Jesus Christ. It is only through faith in Him that we can find true identity and fulfillment. The call of the Gospel is not to condemn those who engage in homosexual practices but to invite them to turn to Jesus Christ and find redemption and transformation.

Let's Make It a Conversation!

1. How has the Christian community approached the issue of homosexuality in the past, and how effective has this approach been?
2. What is your reaction to the scriptural declaration that homosexuality is a departure from God's intended design for human sexuality?
3. What are your thoughts on the idea that homosexuality is considered sinful alongside disobedience to parents in Romans 1? What should we conclude from this?

4. How does embracing one's identity in Christ provide a solution to the struggles surrounding homosexuality? How does this message offer hope that is different from the finger-pointing we often see in religious circles?

91

Can women be leaders in the church?

Quick Answer

Passages often used to argue against women in leadership, such as 1 Corinthians 14:34–35 and 1 Timothy 2:12, are addressing specific situations in the early Church and not placing a universal restriction on women. Romans 16:7 and 16:1 mention women named Junia and Phoebe in leadership roles within the church, and there are examples of women prophesying in 1 Corinthians 14 and Acts 21:9. The role of prophesying in the New Testament era includes speaking to the church for its "edification and exhortation and consolation" (1 Corinthians 14:3)—a role typically carried out by church leaders. The Church should recognize and embrace the gifts and talents of women and allow them to fully participate and serve in the Body of Christ.

Diving Deeper

The idea that women should not speak or serve in church is a common one, but it's not supported by Scripture. In fact, when we look at the passages often used to argue against women in leadership, we see they're addressing specific situations in the early Church, and not making a universal restriction for all time.

In 1 Corinthians 14:34–35, the women were likely seated far away from the men and would shout their questions to their husbands on the other side of the room, causing a disturbance in the church service. Paul was simply addressing the need for orderly worship by instructing wives to ask their husbands these questions at home instead of in the middle of the church service.

In 1 Timothy 2:12, women were seeking to exercise authority over men, likely due to the influence of the cult of Diana, which taught that females were inherently superior to males. This cult also taught that Eve was created first, that Eve was not deceived by Satan, and that women should not bother with marriage and raising children. This is precisely why, in the same passage, Paul says, "Adam was first created, and then Eve"; "it was not Adam who was first deceived, but the woman being deceived"; and that "women will be preserved through the bearing of children" (1 Timothy 2:12–15).

In both 1 Corinthians 14 and 1 Timothy 2, Paul was addressing specific issues in the early Church, not placing a universal restriction on women speaking or serving. And when we look at the rest of Scripture, we see no evidence that women are forbidden from being pastors, elders, or deacons. In fact, there are multiple examples of women in leadership in the New Testament. Romans 16:7 mentions a woman named Junia being a fellow prisoner with Paul because of her work with the Gospel. Romans 16:1 speaks of a deaconess named Phoebe who was central to the work of the Church. Women are also shown to be prophesying in 1 Corinthians 14, and Acts 21:9 states that Philip the evangelist had four daughters who prophesied.

It's important to note that the role of prophesying in the early Church was not about predicting the future, but involved speaking to the Church for its "edification and exhortation and consolation" (1 Corinthians 14:3–4)—a role typically carried out by church leaders. This means that not only were women participating in the church, but they were also fulfilling important roles in its leadership and ministry.

In conclusion, Scripture does not support the idea that women should not speak or serve in church. The passages often used to argue against women in leadership roles are addressing specific situations in the early Church, and there are multiple examples of women in leadership throughout the New Testament. It's time for the Church to recognize and embrace the gifts and talents of women and allow them to fully participate and serve in the Body of Christ.

Let's Make It a Conversation!

1. How do you believe the role of women in the church has been traditionally viewed? Have you ever questioned this perspective?
2. How do the historical and cultural contexts of Corinth and Ephesus shape your understanding of the passages in 1 Corinthians 14:34–35 and 1 Timothy 2:12 that appear to restrict women's roles in the church?

3. How do you think Galatians 3:28, which states that in the Kingdom "there is neither male nor female; for you are all one in Christ Jesus," should inform our perspective on women in the Church?

4. How do the examples of leaders in the New Testament such as Junia, Phoebe, and female prophets impact your understanding of women's roles in the Church?

TRUE AND FALSE BELIEFS

92

Is the Trinity a biblical concept?

Quick Answer

Although not explicitly mentioned in the Bible, the concept of the Trinity is clearly present throughout Scripture. The unity of Father, Son, and Holy Spirit as three coequal persons in one Godhead is evident in the Old Testament, such as in Genesis 1:26, where God speaks in the plural form, "Let Us make mankind in Our image." The New Testament provides even more clarity for the Trinity, with Jesus praying to His Father in John 17 and claiming they are one, and the Apostle Paul describing the Spirit of Christ in Galatians 4:6. Additionally, in Matthew 3:16–17, Jesus's baptism is accompanied by the descent of the Spirit of God and a voice from Heaven declaring Jesus as the Son of God. Furthermore, in Matthew 28:19, Jesus instructs His disciples to baptize in the name of the Father, Son, and Holy Spirit, and in 2 Corinthians 13:14, Paul writes about the grace of Jesus Christ, the love of God, and the fellowship of the Holy Spirit. These verses, among many others, serve as evidence for the Trinity, which is central to the Christian faith.

Diving Deeper

The concept of the Trinity refers to the fact that there is one God who exists in three persons: the Father, the Son, and the Holy Spirit. This belief is not explicitly mentioned (by name) in the Bible, but it is implied throughout the Old and New Testaments.

In the Old Testament, several verses suggest the existence of the Trinity. For example, in Genesis 1:26, God speaks in the plural form, saying "Let Us make mankind in Our image." This communicates that there are multiple persons within the Godhead. Additionally, in Isaiah 48:16, it is written that the Lord God sends forth His Spirit and declares His Word. This passage also conveys the presence of multiple persons within the Godhead.

The New Testament provides even more clarity for the Trinity, with Jesus praying to His Father and claiming they are one in John 17, and Paul describing the Spirit of Christ in Galatians 4:6. These verses demonstrate that Jesus and the Spirit are distinct persons within the Godhead, but they are also one in essence and purpose.

Furthermore, in Matthew 3:16–17, Jesus's baptism is accompanied by the descent of the Spirit of God and a voice from Heaven declaring Jesus as the Son of God. This verse offers evidence for the Trinity and the unity of the three persons of the Godhead. Additionally, in Matthew 28:19, Jesus instructs His disciples to baptize in the name of the Father, Son, and Holy Spirit. This verse gives further evidence for the Trinity and the unity of the three persons of the Godhead. Likewise, in 2 Corinthians 13:14, Paul writes about the grace of Jesus Christ, the love of God, and the fellowship of the Holy Spirit. This conveys the unity of the three persons of the Trinity.

In conclusion, the concept of the Trinity is not explicitly mentioned in the Bible, but it is clearly present throughout Scripture. The unity of Father, Son, and Holy Spirit as three coequal persons in one Godhead is evident in both the Old and New Testament. These passages serve as evidence for the Trinity, which is essential to understanding the nature of God.

Let's Make It a Conversation!

1. Can you share different ways in which you have learned about the concept of the Trinity? How does each explanation compare in terms of making sense to you? Are there any specific aspects of the Trinity that you find difficult to understand or accept?

2. How do you feel about the idea that the Trinity dwells within us (John 14:23)? What are the implications of this belief, and how might it shape our understanding of ourselves and our relationship with God?

3. React to this statement: The entire Trinity is pleased to have you. Wherever you go, you're never alone. There's always Father, Son, Holy Spirit . . . and you!

93
Did Jesus spend three days in Hell?

Quick Answer

The Bible does not teach that Jesus descended into Hell for three days after His death on the cross. Instead, passages such as Luke 23:43 and Hebrews 10:14 suggest that Jesus's death was a sufficient sacrifice for our sins, and that He went to "paradise" (Heaven) immediately after His death. This is supported by the use of the Greek word *phylakē* in 1 Peter 3:19 as a reference to the realm of the dead and the context of the passage which suggests that Jesus proclaimed His victory over sin and death. The idea of Jesus suffering in Hell for three days is not found in the New Testament and is a later interpretation of 1 Peter 3:19.

Diving Deeper

The idea that Jesus spent three days in Hell was popularized by the worldwide recitation of the Apostle's Creed. However, the phrase about His descent into Hell was not present in the earliest versions of the Apostles' Creed, such as the Old Roman Symbol, which dates to the second or third century. This version, also known as the Old Roman Creed, is one of the earliest forms of the Apostles' Creed. The absence of the descent into Hell has led scholars to argue the phrase was added later (around the fourth or fifth century).

Furthermore, the Bible does not teach that Jesus descended into Hell for three days after His death on the cross. Instead, several passages of Scripture indicate that Jesus went to Paradise or Heaven immediately after His death. Luke 23:43 states that Jesus told the thief on the cross, "Today you shall be with Me in paradise." This statement suggests that Jesus went to Paradise immediately after His death and did not descend

TRUE AND FALSE BELIEFS

into Hell. Some might wonder why Jesus told Mary not to hang on to Him (John 20:17). Was it a reference to Him needing to go to Hell first? No, He actually said, "Stop clinging to me for I have not yet ascended to the Father" (John 20:17). He wanted Mary to recognize the importance of His ascension and the coming Holy Spirit—a relationship with Him that would be better than the present one.

Additionally, the Bible teaches that Jesus's death on the cross was a sufficient sacrifice for the sins of humanity. Hebrews 10:14 states that "by one offering He has made perfect for all time those who are sanctified." This indicates that Jesus's death was a perfect sacrifice that fully deals with our sins and makes us holy in the eyes of God. It does not suggest that any additional work, such as preaching in Hell, was necessary to complete the work of God on our behalf.

First Peter 3:19, which is sometimes used as evidence of Jesus's descent into Hell, should be understood in a different way. The passage states that Jesus "made proclamation to the spirits now in prison." Some interpret this to mean that Jesus descended into Hell to preach to the unsaved, but this is not the meaning of the passage. The context is a comparison between the preaching of Jesus and the preaching of Noah. Therefore, it is more likely that Peter is saying Jesus (through the preaching of Noah) testified to the impending judgment of God. Note that Peter calls Noah a "preacher of righteousness" (2 Peter 2:5). Noah preached in the power of the Holy Spirit whom Peter earlier calls "the Spirit of Christ" (1 Peter 1:11).

But the people of Noah's generation rejected Noah's message (and therefore, Jesus's message through Noah). And because of their rejection of it, they are now in a spiritual prison (Hell).

In conclusion, the Bible does not teach that Jesus descended into Hell for three days after His death on the cross. Instead, passages such as Luke 23:43 and Hebrews 10:14 suggest that Jesus's death was a sufficient sacrifice for our sins, and that His spirit went to Heaven immediately after His death. Furthermore, the interpretation of 1 Peter 3:19 as Jesus preaching in Hell is not an accurate understanding of the passage. Instead, it is referring to Jesus preaching through Noah (in the days of Noah) and His hearers being in prison (Hell) now as a result of rejecting the message of God.

Let's Make It a Conversation!

1. Have you ever heard that Jesus descended into Hell for three days after His death on the cross? What are your thoughts on this belief?

2. How do you interpret 1 Peter 3:18–20 in light of the discussion here on whether or not it references Jesus descending into Hell?

3. What does recognizing that Jesus did *not* descend into Hell for three days after His death contribute to your understanding of the sufficiency of His death on the cross?

94
Should we follow the "early Church fathers"?

Quick Answer

Some argue that we should adhere to what the "early Church fathers" taught during the first few centuries of Christianity. While this might sound like a noble idea, it is problematic in that the early Church fathers did not even agree with each other about key issues. Furthermore, many of the so-called "early Church fathers" promoted unfounded (even heretical!) ideas. In short, it's not the age of a belief that determines its truth value. What's most important is what the Scriptures actually teach, not what those who came later might have claimed. And the Spirit of God is perfectly capable of teaching us the truth of the Gospel today, so we have no need to blindly submit to the ideas proposed by the "early Church fathers."

Diving Deeper

Adhering to the teachings of the "early Church fathers" during the first few centuries of Christianity might sound like a noble idea, but they did not even agree with each other about key issues of doctrine. Furthermore, many of the so-called "early Church fathers" promoted heretical ideas. For example, Origen believed in the ultimate reconciliation of all people through Christ, while Tertullian believed people should be baptized on their deathbeds to ensure their salvation was secured. Irenaeus, on the other hand, believed that Old Testament Gentiles were justified by living according to Greek philosophy. Thus, if we were to simply follow the early Church fathers, we would have quite an odd theological compilation!

In addition, the "early Church fathers" often had different cultural backgrounds, leading to different perspectives. For example, Ignatius of Antioch, who lived in the early second century, had a different approach to church leadership than Cyprian of Carthage, who lived in the mid-third century. Also, many of the teachings and beliefs of the "early Church fathers" were influenced by the politics of their time. For example, they were influenced by the Greeks and the Romans, which led to the incorporation of some philosophy and even political ideas into their theology.

Paul warned in Colossians 2:8 that we should not be taken captive to "philosophy and empty deception" which depends on the "tradition of men" instead of Christ. The early Church fathers were fallible human beings just like us, and it doesn't take long for people to distort the Gospel message. Consider the church in Corinth that was abusing the Lord's Supper and getting things wrong very early, or the Galatians who were mandating circumcision and Law-keeping, thereby also getting things wrong very early.

The bottom line is that the age of a belief does not determine its truth value. The Holy Spirit is perfectly capable of teaching us the truth of the Gospel today, so we have no need to blindly submit to ideas proposed by the "early Church fathers." Instead, we should rely on the guidance of the Holy Spirit and the teachings of the Scripture, which are the ultimate authorities in determining our beliefs.

In summary, the idea of adhering to the teachings of the "early Church fathers" is problematic, because they didn't always agree with each other on key issues of doctrine. Some of their ideas were even heretical. It's more important to base our beliefs on what the Scriptures teach rather than relying on the interpretations of fallible human beings. Additionally, even within the early Church, there were already examples of people distorting the Gospel message. This highlights the importance of being discerning and not blindly accepting the teachings of any one person or group. Ultimately, we should rely on the guidance of the Holy Spirit to lead us to a deeper understanding of the truth found in the Scriptures.

Let's Make It a Conversation!

1. Can you share any examples of early Church fathers and their differing beliefs on key issues of doctrine? How do these differences affect your understanding of the early Church and how quickly they got off base?

2. How do you think basing our theology on tradition can be problematic? Can you provide examples? How can we ensure that we are not being taken captive by "hollow and deceptive philosophy" that depends on human traditions?

3. In light of the potential issues with basing our theology on tradition, what are some ways we can ensure that we are adhering to the true gospel of grace as outlined in Acts 20:24? How can we rely on the guidance of the Holy Spirit and the teachings of the Scriptures to deepen our understanding of the truth of the Gospel?

95

Do you go straight to Heaven when you die?

Quick Answer

Scripture makes it clear that when believers die, they enter the presence of God and are not in an intermediate state waiting for Jesus's return. The Apostle Paul believed that upon his death, he would be with Jesus (2 Corinthians 5:8; Philippians 1:23), and Jesus promised the thief on the cross that same day he would be together with Jesus in Heaven (Luke 23:43). The Bible also teaches that death is a "departure" from one's earthly body and an entering into the presence of the Lord (2 Corinthians 5:6–8; Philippians 1:21–24). Believers are resurrected and receive new bodies at the second coming of Christ, and only an understanding of eternity—after we leave time as we know it—can inform us of whether the receiving of that body feels immediate or not. But we can have confidence that upon death, we'll be with Jesus in Heaven instantly and not waiting in some intermediate state.

Diving Deeper

When we die, we believers enter the presence of God immediately. Scripture is clear that to die is to be present with the Lord (2 Corinthians 5:8; Luke 23:43). The Apostle Paul believed wholeheartedly that he would be with Jesus when he died (2 Corinthians 5:8; Philippians 1:23). And Jesus promised the thief on the cross that he would be with Him in Paradise the moment he died (Luke 23:43). This is a powerful and comforting message for us, as it means that our believing loved ones who pass away are with Jesus right away.

So death is a departure from one's earthly body and an entrance into the presence of the Lord (2 Corinthians 5:6–8; Philippians 1:21–24). However, some teach that believers enter an intermediate state when they die, waiting for Jesus to return to Earth and usher in the new heavens and new Earth. This idea can be confusing for those who live on Earth in time, as it suggests that there is a waiting period between death and eternal life. But it's important to remember that God is outside of time, so everything is "right now" for Him. So when you die, Heaven will be ready for you, and your Savior will be waiting for you.

The Bible also teaches that believers will be resurrected and receive new bodies at the second coming of Christ. This idea can also be confusing, as it might suggest to some that believers are not fully alive in the presence of God and may be waiting to receive their new bodies. But this is not the case. Believers are fully alive in the presence of God, enjoying eternal life, and upon death we may even awaken to the sound of a trumpet and receive our new bodies. Eternity is a mystery, and currently we are time-creatures, so it remains unclear which "point" in eternity we enter upon death.

In conclusion, the Bible teaches that when believers die, they immediately enter the presence of God. Death is not a waiting period for us, but an immediate entrance into a heavenly life with Jesus forever. Death is like falling asleep and immediately awakening to a whole new experience. As a

Christian, you can be confident that when you die, you will be with Him right away and not waiting. This is a message of hope and comfort we can share to bring peace and reassurance to believers in difficult times. It reminds us that death is not the end, but a continuation of the eternal life we *already* enjoy in Jesus Christ.

Let's Make It a Conversation!

1. How does the biblical imagery of death as a "sleep" shape our understanding of it and the afterlife?
2. What are the implications of God being outside of time in eternity for our understanding of "when" we get our new bodies?
3. How can the understanding that death is simply a transition bring comfort and reassurance to believers in difficult times?
4. How can reflecting on the teachings of the Bible about Heaven and the afterlife impact the way we think about life on Earth?

96

What is the concept of Lordship Salvation?

Quick Answer

"Lordship Salvation" emphasizes the importance of obedience and good works as proof of genuine faith. This doctrine has been criticized as problematic due to its emphasis on one's own efforts and dedication rather than solely on grace, which can lead to confusion, self-doubt, and works-based salvation. True assurance of salvation is found in understanding that it's a free gift, not earned, and by simply examining if Christ lives within us as stated in 2 Corinthians 13:5. Lordship Salvation proponents criticize salvation by "easy believism." But Jesus told us what He offers is easy and light (Matthew 11:28–30) and that whoever believes in Him (even those who believe in His name) will be saved (John 3:16; John 1:12). Apparently, "easy believism" is indeed the path to salvation, and we should embrace it as the Gospel presents it. Lordship Salvation is a crippling doctrine that causes morbid introspection and hinders the assurance of salvation.

Diving Deeper

Lordship Salvation is a hot topic in the world of theology, and it's important to get to the bottom of what it really means. This doctrine says that in order to be saved, we not only need to believe in Jesus as our Savior, but also surrender to Him as Lord, making Him the ruler of our lives. In other words, it's not just about saying a prayer, but also about obedience and good works as evidence of genuine faith.

But here's the thing: Lordship Salvation is a trap! It can lead to constant self-analysis, wondering if we've surrendered enough or if our motives are pure enough. This can bring doubt to true believers who have already called on the name of the Lord for salvation. And that's not healthy.

Let's look at the Bible. Romans 6:23 says that the "wages of sin is death, but the free gift of God is eternal life in Christ

Jesus our Lord." This clearly states that salvation is a free gift, not something we earn through works or effort.

And yet, Lordship Salvation can seem like a works-based salvation. It emphasizes our actions and efforts, rather than the grace of God and belief in Jesus as the Son of God. This goes against the teachings of the Bible, like Ephesians 2:8–9, which says,

> For by grace you have been saved through faith; and that not of yourselves, it is the gift of God; not as a result of works, so that no one may boast.

Jesus Himself spoke against the idea of Lordship Salvation when He said,

> "Come to Me, all who are weary and heavy-laden, and I will give you rest. Take My yoke upon you and learn from Me, for I am gentle and humble in heart, and you will find rest for your souls. For My yoke is easy and My burden is light." (Matthew 11:28–30)

He wants salvation to be easy for us, not a heavy burden. And He said in John 3:16 and John 1:12 that whoever believes in Him has eternal life.

In conclusion, Lordship Salvation sows doubt in the minds of true believers. The seeds of doubt sown might look something this: "Did I truly surrender? Did I repent enough?

Did I actually make Christ the Lord of my life? Maybe I made Him Savior but not Lord!"

Lordship Salvation is a doctrine that teaches that individuals are saved only when they "fully" surrender and submit to Christ's Lordship. This can lead to doubt and introspection, hindering the assurance of salvation. It is a problematic doctrine that is ultimately rooted in "faith plus works as evidence for assurance" rather than salvation by grace through faith alone. The Bible clearly states that salvation is a free gift and not something that is verified through enough works or enough "surrender."

Let's Make It a Conversation!

1. Had you ever heard about the doctrine of "Lordship Salvation"? What are your thoughts on it? How does it differ from biblical beliefs about salvation?

2. How do you respond to the idea that someone can make Jesus their Savior but not their Lord? By calling on Jesus to save us, doesn't this assume He has the power and authority ("Lordship") to do so, and we're submitting to Him to save us?

3. What do you think about salvation being offered freely and received by simply calling upon the name of the Lord? Consider the thief on the cross who had no time to put his faith into action or prove his repentance to be genuine. How does this relate to the false ideas in Lordship Salvation?

97

Is Catholicism the one true faith?

Quick Answer

Catholicism is not the one true expression of the Christian faith. Catholicism teaches that we need priests to serve as intermediaries between us and God, but the New Testament says Jesus is the only Mediator and that all believers have direct access to God through faith in Him. Catholicism says sacraments are how we receive God's grace, but the New Testament teaches that grace is received through faith in Jesus alone. Catholicism carries a strong devotion to Mary, but there is no scriptural basis for praying to her or anyone besides God; she was a human, not a deity. Catholicism venerates certain individuals as saints, but the Bible says all believers are saints and salvation is through grace alone, not through any religious institution. The Bible clearly teaches that salvation is by grace through faith alone, while Catholicism emphasizes faith plus good works as the means to salvation.

Diving Deeper

It's inaccurate to say Catholicism is the one true expression of the Christian faith. This idea is problematic because it suggests that salvation is only attainable through the Catholic Church.

The Catholic Church's teaching that priests serve as intermediaries between God and humanity contradicts the New Testament, which teaches that Jesus Christ is the only

Mediator (1 Timothy 2:5). The Bible also says all believers are part of a royal priesthood of God (1 Peter 2:9) and that Jesus is our High Priest (Hebrews 4:15). We have a *direct* relationship with God through faith in Jesus Christ.

According to Catholicism, we receive God's grace through participating in sacraments like the Lord's Supper. However, the New Testament teaches that grace is received through faith in Jesus alone. Catholicism also believes in the doctrine of transubstantiation, the idea that the Lord's Supper literally becomes Jesus's body and blood. The New Testament, however, describes the Lord's Supper as a symbolic celebration carried out in remembrance of Jesus's death (1 Corinthians 11:24).

The Catholic Church places an emphasis on Mary, with practices like the rosary and Hail Mary prayer. However, the New Testament does not instruct us to pray to Mary or anyone else besides God. All believers have already been redeemed by Christ and have direct access to God, so there is no need for any mediator besides Jesus Christ.

Finally, Catholicism recognizes certain individuals as saints, but only if they meet the Catholic Church's standards. However, the Bible says all believers are saints, as they have been forgiven, made holy, and adopted into God's family (1 Corinthians 1:2; Romans 1:7; Hebrews 10:10, 14; 1 John 3:1). Salvation comes by the grace of God through Christ, not through any religious institution.

In conclusion, Catholicism's teachings on intermediaries, sacraments, the veneration of Mary, and sainthood are at odds with a biblical understanding. The New Testament teaches that Jesus is the only Mediator, grace is received through faith in Him alone, prayer should only be directed to God, and all believers are saints. Salvation comes through faith in Jesus as our Savior, while Catholicism emphasizes a combination of faith, good works, and sacraments.

Let's Make It a Conversation!

1. How does your understanding of salvation compare to the Catholic understanding?
2. What Scripture supports the belief that Jesus is the only Mediator between God and humanity?
3. How are the Catholic views of the Lord's Supper and Mary a departure from Scripture?
4. What does the Bible teach about being a saint? How does this compare to the Catholic doctrine of canonizing only certain believers as saints?

98

Is the King James Version of the Bible superior to others?

Quick Answer

The claim that the King James Version is the most accurate translation of the Bible is problematic for several reasons. Firstly, it was written more than 1,600 years after the writing of the New Testament, and a few thousand years after the penning of the Old Testament began. Secondly, it is not based on the earliest manuscripts available, and today we have access to many other manuscripts that help us better understand the original texts. Additionally, it has been criticized for its use of archaic language and translation errors, and its creation was influenced by political and cultural factors of the time. Therefore, limiting ourselves to the King James Version only is to limit our understanding of Scripture. It's important to remember that the Bible is a "living text," and as such, it should be approached with an open mind and a willingness to explore different translations.

Diving Deeper

The King James Version of the Bible is often touted as the most accurate translation of the Scriptures; however, this claim is problematic for several reasons. Firstly, the translation was written more than 1,600 years after the writing of the New Testament, and a few thousand years after the penning of the Old Testament began. This means that the translation is based on much later versions of the text, which can introduce inaccuracies and misunderstandings.

Secondly, the King James Version is not based on the earliest manuscripts available. It largely utilizes translations constructed by Erasmus (*Textus Receptus*) for the New Testament and the Masoretic Hebrew text for the Old Testament. Today, we have access to many other manuscripts that help us better understand the original Greek and Hebrew writings. These manuscripts have been discovered in recent years and have been translated using advanced techniques and tools that were not available at the time of the King James Version.

Thirdly, it is problematic to claim that, out of all of the languages in existence and all the translations from these languages, God prefers the King James Version. Millions of believers in China, for example, have no interest in any English translation. The idea that the KJV is the best translation is a Western idea formulated on an English-speaking continent.

Additionally, the King James Version has been criticized for its use of archaic language, which can make it difficult for modern readers to understand. Furthermore, it contains translation errors that were not corrected until later versions. These errors include mistranslations of the Greek *agape* (love) as "charity" in 1 Corinthians 13:4 and the Greek word *baptizo* (immersion) as "wash" in Mark 7:4. Additionally, the Greek word *huios* (son) was mistranslated as "servant" in Matthew 12:18. These are just a few among many errors in the history of the King James Version.

It's also important to note that the King James Version was not created in a vacuum. It was commissioned by King James I of England and was heavily influenced by the political and cultural factors of the time. This means that the translation is not only based on a later version of the text, but also a version that has been influenced by the biases and perspectives of the translators.

In summary, while the King James Version has played an important role in the history of the English language and Christian theology, it's not the most accurate translation of the Bible. Today, we have access to many more manuscripts and translations that help us better understand the original texts. By reading multiple translations, we can gain a more nuanced understanding of the Bible and its message.

Let's Make It a Conversation!

1. Have you ever encountered someone who believes that the King James Version is the only accurate translation of the Bible? If so, what were their reasons for this belief?

2. What are some of the reasons that people may be drawn to elevating one translation or version of the Bible above all others?

3. How do you think reading multiple versions of the Bible can enhance our understanding of its message?

99

What does "by His wounds we are healed" mean?

Quick Answer

While Isaiah 53:5 is interpreted by some to mean that Christians have guaranteed physical healing through the finished work of Christ, the passage is actually speaking of a spiritual healing which occurs at salvation (1 Peter 2:24). This healing is not physical but spiritual—the forgiveness of sins and the righteousness we receive in Christ. As believers, we pray for physical healing, but it's crucial to remember that not everyone is healed in this life. God's ultimate plan for believers is eternal life in Heaven. Of course, God does perform miracles, but physical healing should not be expected as a guaranteed outcome of the cross. Trust in God's whole plan for our lives, which includes the promise of a new resurrection body in Heaven.

Diving Deeper

Isaiah 53:5 speaks of the healing that Christ's death and resurrection brings to believers. This healing is not physical, but spiritual—the forgiveness of sins and the bestowment of righteousness in Christ. In 1 Peter 2:24, Peter directly links this healing to the forgiveness of sins, emphasizing its spiritual nature.

The Apostle Paul thanked the early Church for taking care of him when he was ill (Galatians 4:14). Paul departed from Miletus while Trophimus was sick and offered him no remedy (2 Timothy 4:20). Timothy had frequent stomach ailments, and Paul suggested he take some red wine to help (1 Timothy 5:23). Clearly, no one should be teaching a guaranteed healing for all Christians through the finished work of Christ. Such a doctrine is nowhere to be found in the New Testament, and it only sets people up for unrealistic expectations and disappointment with God.

While it's important to pray for physical healing, we must be careful not to have these misaligned expectations of guaranteed physical healing. Not everyone is healed in this life, and God's ultimate goal for believers is life with Him forever in Heaven. God's ways are higher than our understanding of them.

God performs miracles, including physical healing, but these are not a guaranteed outcome of the finished work of Christ. Instead, we can trust in God's plan and purpose for our lives, knowing that whatever happens, God is working everything for our ultimate good and for His glory. God is good.

In conclusion, Isaiah 53:5 and other passages that some people interpret as guaranteeing physical healing must be understood in context to mean that Jesus took the punishment for our sins so that we wouldn't have to—"by His wounds we are healed" (NIV). While God performs miracles, including physical healing, these should not be expected as a guaranteed outcome of salvation. Instead, we must trust in God's ultimate plan for our lives, which includes a perfect resurrection body. This is the ultimate answer to any physical ailments we experience now.

Let's Make It a Conversation!

1. How might a misinterpretation of Isaiah 53:5 lead to unrealistic expectations and disappointment in terms of healing?
2. Can you share an example of how you have personally experienced healing (spiritual, emotional, or physical) through Jesus?
3. React to this statement: Every single person who has taught guaranteed physical healing ends up dying like the rest of us.

100

What is "the prosperity gospel"?

Quick Answer

The prosperity gospel is a false teaching that promises believers wealth (and health) if they have enough faith. However, the Bible teaches that Christ's death, burial, and resurrection guarantee us spiritual blessings such as forgiveness, righteousness, and a new heart. These are the true gifts of God, which belong to every believer. The prosperity gospel preys on the vulnerable, leaving them feeling guilty and ashamed when the promises fail to come true. It's important to understand that the Bible is filled with examples of believers who suffered physically and financially yet lived godly and fulfilled lives. We must reject the prosperity gospel and cling to the true message of the Gospel, which is the good news of guaranteed spiritual salvation right now and guaranteed physical deliverance in Heaven.

Diving Deeper

The prosperity gospel is one of the most dangerous and deceptive teachings to infiltrate the modern church. It teaches that Christ's death, burial, and resurrection brought every believer the ability to activate earthly blessings such as monetary riches and good health. However, this is a gross misrepresentation of the true message of the Gospel. Scripture teaches that Christ achieved spiritual blessings for us such as forgiveness, righteousness, and a new heart (Ephesians 1; Hebrews 10:16–17). These are the true gifts of God which belong to every believer regardless of what Planet Earth might throw our way.

The prosperity gospel claims that Christ's death, burial, and resurrection guarantee us physical healing and/or financial wealth if we have enough faith. However, it doesn't take long to realize this spiritual formula simply does not work. Perhaps you lose your job, or you get sick, even after you've "named and claimed" prosperity and health. The prosperity gospel consistently falls short as a tenable theology.

The prosperity gospel might sound nice, but it simply doesn't work in the real world. Christ's death, burial, and resurrection guarantee our salvation from start to finish (Ephesians 1; Hebrews 8:8–12; Hebrews 10:16–17). When we believe the Gospel, we are given spiritual blessings as a free gift (Ephesians 1:3). Jesus Christ Himself dwells within us, and the love of God is poured into our hearts (Romans 5:5). Now that's true prosperity!

The prosperity gospel is not only false, it's dangerous. It preys on the vulnerable, promising them wealth and health if they just have enough faith. But when these promises fail to come to fruition, it leaves people feeling like they've failed God and that they are being punished. This kind of false teaching can lead to feelings of guilt, shame, and even despair.

The proponents of the prosperity gospel often cite passages such as 3 John 1:2 which says, "Beloved, I pray that in all respects you may prosper and be in good health, just as your soul prospers." But it's important to understand that this verse is not a promise of physical health and wealth. It is simply a prayer for the well-being of the believer. The Bible is filled with examples of believers who suffered physically and financially yet still lived victorious and fulfilled lives.

Neither Jesus nor the apostles were wealthy. Jesus had no place to lay His head (Luke 9:58), and many of the apostles were tortured and killed with no belongings to their name. Furthermore, the Apostle Paul was sick and thanked the Galatians for taking care of him. He also prescribed red wine for Timothy's frequent stomach ailments (1 Timothy 5:23). Clearly, wealth and health were not "activated" in the lives of early believers.

We should reject the prosperity gospel and cling to the true Gospel, which is the good news of salvation through Jesus Christ.

Let's Make It a Conversation!

1. What has been your exposure to the prosperity gospel?
2. React to this statement: Neither Jesus nor the apostles were wealthy.
3. How does the concept of contentment in Philippians 4:12 relate to the false promises of the prosperity gospel?

101
What does "I can do all things through Christ" really mean?

Quick Answer
Many people think Philippians 4:13 is a magic formula for success in life. Like, if you just have Jesus on your team, you can accomplish anything! But that's not exactly what this verse is all about. No, it's actually about finding peace and contentment in any situation, whether you're living the high life or barely scraping by. The Apostle Paul is actually saying that Jesus is your strength, no matter what you might experience on Earth. He's your comfort, no matter how much or how little you have. So, don't think of this verse as a promise that you'll be a millionaire or a president just because you have Jesus on your side. Think of it as a promise that you'll be okay, no matter what circumstances you may face.

Diving Deeper
Many people interpret Philippians 4:13 as a promise of success and victory for Christians in any and every aspect of life. They believe that because they have Jesus in their lives, they can accomplish anything they set their minds to. However, this interpretation is not entirely accurate. The passage is actually about something much deeper and more profound: contentment and the ability to find peace and fulfillment in any circumstance, whether we're experiencing abundance or scarcity, success or failure.

The Apostle Paul writes about having little and having much, going hungry and being filled. But he doesn't do so to suggest that Christians can achieve anything they set their minds to with the help of Jesus. Instead, he's pointing to the fact that Jesus is our life, our source of strength and comfort, in every situation we encounter. He's saying that through Jesus Christ's power within him, he has learned the secret of contentment in every circumstance.

It's easy to fall into the trap of thinking that if we simply declare our faith in Jesus, we'll be able to achieve all of our wildest dreams. But that's not what the Bible teaches. Instead, it teaches us that we can endure any hardship, because Jesus lives within us and gives us the strength to do so. It's not a passage about chasing the "American Dream" through Jesus. It's about the stability in Christ and the counsel of God's Spirit that we enjoy even when our ambitions fail.

In conclusion, Philippians 4:13 is not a promise of worldly success, but a promise of contentment and fulfillment in any circumstance. It reminds us that our strength and peace come from Jesus and that we can find contentment in Him, regardless of what life throws at us. It's a reminder that through the power of Jesus Christ, we can *endure* anything.

Let's Make It a Conversation!

1. How do you think our society's emphasis on success and achievement might impact our understanding of Philippians 4:13? How might our personal experiences—

whether succeeding or failing—also play a role in how we feel about this verse?

2. In your own words, what do you believe the verse is truly conveying? How does this understanding change the way we approach challenges and hardships in life?

3. Have you ever found yourself relying on the strength of Christ to endure a difficult situation? How did it impact your perspective and approach to the challenge? How might your experience equip you to encourage someone else who's going through a tough time?

Acknowledgments

I am deeply grateful and indebted to my dear friends, Andrew Nelson and Jane Bromley, for their unwavering dedication and hard work in assisting me with the collection and transcription of my audio answers. Without their invaluable research, brainstorming, and early contributions, the BibleQuestions.com website and the resulting book would not have been possible. Andrew and Jane's tireless efforts and commitment to this project were truly indispensable, and I am forever grateful.

Furthermore, I would like to express my heartfelt appreciation to my exceptional editor, Karla Dial, whose insightful feedback and suggestions have significantly enhanced the quality and impact of this book. Her meticulous attention to detail and expert guidance have been instrumental in bringing this project to fruition. Thank you, Karla, for your invaluable contributions and unwavering support.

Lastly, I want to extend my deepest gratitude to my wife, Katharine, and our son, Gavin, for their love and support throughout the writing process. Your encouragement and understanding have sustained me through the long hours and challenging moments. I am truly blessed to have you both in my life, and I love you more than words can express. Thank you for being a constant source of strength and inspiration.

More books by Andrew Farley

The Naked Gospel
God Without Religion
Heaven is Now
The Art of Spiritual War
The Hurt & The Healer
Relaxing with God
Twisted Scripture
The Perfect You
The Grace Message

Podcasts by Andrew Farley

The Grace Message
The Good Call
Foundations of Faith

Follow Andrew on social media

@DrAndrewFarley

Websites

AndrewFarley.org
BibleQuestions.com
BibleCommentary.org
TheGraceChurch.org

Mobile app

Andrew Farley (The Grace Message)